Japan

More than any other equally wealthy and complex country, Japan has the capacity to arouse wonder. The frantic lives of the residents, the monolithic social structure, the highly original culture industry, the gigantic technology corporations, the resilient traditions and the many and varied subcultures in its post-human mega-cities leave foreigners either in awe or disturbed and turn them into ethnologists scratching their perplexed heads. So it is hardly surprising that since time immemorial countless travellers, enthusiasts, reporters and writers have poured out rivers of ink over this unique country. Isn't amazement one of the fuels of good literature? More or less untranslatable words, once deciphered by the Rising Sun-besotted nerd of the day, are now a part of our common culture – *otaku, karōshi, sararīman, shokunin, gōkon* – but Japan remains rather like a jigsaw puzzle, one which we can assemble in part but whose overall pattern remains obscure. This has given rise to endless stories, tales and observations, such as those you can read in the coming pages of this inevitably subjective but eclectic collection: from ancestor worship to the Tokyo music scene, from urban alienation to film, from sumo to male chauvinism to mention a few. Japan, suspended between an ageing population and extreme post-modernity, between opposition to progress and futuristic experimentation, is an ideal vantage point from which to see the world as it is today and as it will become tomorrow. That is, provided we embark on this journey without any expectation of solving the mystery because, as Brian Phillips reminds us in 'Sea of Crises' (see page 99): 'Some Japanese stories end violently. Others never end at all but only cut away, at the moment of extreme crisis, to a butterfly or the wind or the moon.'

Contents

Japan in Numbers — 6
The Mythbuster — Tania Palmieri — 8
The Number — Matteo Battarra — 10

Ghosts of the Tsunami — Richard Lloyd Parry — 13
  The devastating 2011 tsunami reinvigorated the ancestor cult, Japan's true religion. Survivors still report mysterious apparitions and disturbing cases of possession. We meet Reverend Kaneta, who offers spiritual help both to the possessed and the suffering souls taking possession of them.

The 'Do-it-Yourself' Women — Sekiguchi Ryōko — 35
  Having liberated themselves from the role of housewife and entering the world of work, many women are now dreaming of a return to the tranquil profession of 'domestic designer'.

The (No Longer So) Secret Cult that Governs Japan — Jake Adelstein — 45
  A Shinto sect with a monarchic, patriotic and revisionist programme operates in the shadow of political power. Prime Minister Abe Shinzō and other prominent politicians are among its members.

Why Is Japan Populist-Free? — Ian Buruma — 59
  Ian Buruma's optimistic analysis of Japan suggests that, despite Prime Minister Abe Shinzō's nationalism, it remains a country rooted in the middle class in which a kind of social harmony still prevails.

A Simple Thank You — Yoshimoto Banana — 67
  Yoshimoto Banana's love letter to Shimokitazawa, the area of Tokyo where she has lived for many years, provides her with the opportunity to reflect on her memories and changes in contemporary Japan.

The Withering of Desire — Murakami Ryū — 79
  The inability to be moved, the decline in desire and the growth in cases of depression are examined by one of Japan's major writers, who wonders if it is all caused by socio-economic instability.

Of Bears and Men — Cesare Alemanni — 87
  For centuries the Ainu, an ancient people from the island of Hokkaido, have been labelled as a 'prehistoric aberration' and been victims of oppression. Having successfully resisted assimilation thanks to the strength of their traditions, they are now being rediscovered.

Sea of Crises — Brian Phillips 99
A writer's journey to follow the most important tournament in the sumo calendar becomes a voyage into the past as he follows the trail of a forgotten man and a sensational case of seppuku in 1970.

Sweet Bitter Blues — Amanda Petrusich 125
Why are the Japanese so crazy about the blues? The answer seems to have more to do with the nature of Japanese culture than the exoticism of a distinctly African-American musical genre.

Family Album — Giorgio Amitrano 147
A cinematic journey into how families are portrayed in Japanese cinema. From young people struggling to break free of their parents in Ozu Yasujirō's post-war masterpieces through to the indifference of contemporary society and alternative families, we go on a journey that deconstructs the myth of the 'typical' Japanese family.

The Evaporated — Léna Mauger 159
After abruptly disappearing to make a new life elsewhere, tens of thousands of Japanese are living in the shadows to escape debt, an astonishing phenomenon that goes way back to Japan's feudal past.

The Iconic Object — Giacomo Donati 178
The National Obsession — Matteo Battarra 180
The Phenomenon — Cesare Alemanni 182
An Author Recommends — Furukawa Hideo 184
The Playlist — Furukawa Hideo 188
Further Reading 190

The photographs in this issue are by **Laura Liverani**, a documentary photographer and university lecturer who divides her time between Italy and Tokyo. Her pictures provide a fascinating insight into contemporary Japan. She received the Voglino Award for her extensive research into the country's Ainu minority. Her work has been published in *D – la Repubblica*, *Clothes for Humans* by Benetton, *Marie Claire*, *The Washington Post* and *The Japan Times*. She has held personal exhibitions in Tokyo at the Italian Cultural Institute and the G/P Gallery and at the Fringe Club in Hong Kong. She has been invited to numerous international festivals, including the Singapore International Photography Festival, the Festival of Ethnic Photography in Lodi, Italy, and the Indian Photography Festival in Hyderabad. Laura has taught photography at various institutes, including the ISIA in Faenza, Italy, the National College of Art and Design in Dublin, Ireland, and Middlesex University in London, UK.

Japan in Numbers

TIME TO EAT?

Tokyo has more restaurants per head of population than any other city.

Restaurants per 100,000 people

Tokyo	**1,122**
Seoul	806.4
Shenzen	781.7
San Francisco	493.4
Sydney	400.4
Los Angeles	361.5
Brussels	360.4
Rome	333.8
Paris	319.8
Toronto	304.4
London	289.4
New York	287.7
Taipei	261.3

SOURCE: WORLD CITIES CULTURE FORUM

KEEPING IN SHAPE

Adult obesity (% of population) and world ranking

2.1%	**4.3%**	21.6%
Vietnam (1st)	**Japan (7th)**	France (87th)

27.8%	36.2%	61%
UK (157th)	USA (181st)	Nauru (191st)

SOURCE: CIA WORLD FACTBOOK

GENDER EQUALITY

Japan ranks 110th in the WEF Global Gender Gap Report.

Global index and ranking

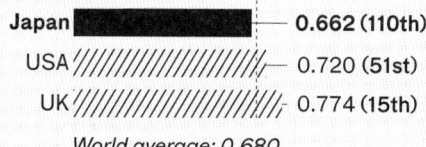

Japan	**0.662 (110th)**
USA	0.720 (51st)
UK	0.774 (15th)

World average: 0.680

SOURCE: WORLD ECONOMIC FORUM

DEBT

Japan leads the world in government debt.

Net government debt as a percentage of GDP

1. Japan — 258
2. Sudan — 207
3. Greece — 177
4. Eritrea — 165
5. Lebanon — 155
6. Italy — 133
13. USA — 106
28. UK — 86

SOURCE: IMF

PERSONAL SPACE

The world's 5 most crowded cities

① Tokyo (37.8m)
② Shanghai (34.8m)
③ Jakarta (31.6m)
④ Delhi (26.4m)
⑤ Seoul (25.5m)

SOURCE: WIKIPEDIA

PEACEFUL

1st

Japan has the world's lowest murder rate.

SOURCE: UNODC

KING OF FRUIT

5

million yen ($45,650 / £34,850)

The price of a couple of Yūbari King melons at auction in 2019; the world's most expensive fruit.

LIFE EXPECTANCY

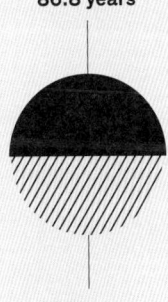

Women
86.8 years

80.5 years
Men

Japan gets the top slot globally, the UK 20th and the USA 37th.

SOURCE: WHO

(NO) TIME FOR SLEEP

Japan ranks last in the world for hours of sleep.

	Estonia	Canada	UK	South Africa	USA	Spain	China	Israel	Japan
Bedtime	00:01	23:30	23:44	22:45	23:26	0:45	0:24	0:07	0:24
Sleep	7h38'	7h29'	7h24'	7h21'	7h21'	7h11'	7h04'	6h48'	6h38'
Wake	7:39	7:02	7:11	6:06	6:52	7:56	7:28	6:55	7:02

SOURCE: POLAR

Japan in Numbers

The Mythbuster

Debunking stereotypes and clichés

TANIA PALMIERI
Translated by Katherine Gregor

1 'The Japanese are aloof.'

It is a well-known fact that the Japanese bow when they greet you. Hugs, kisses on the cheek and handshakes cause embarrassment, as do public displays of affection by couples. We are accustomed to thinking that the Japanese are standoffish and incapable of expressing their feelings and that respect for others takes absolute precedence over the emotional needs of the individual. And yet all we have to do is switch on the television to be presented with the spectacle of public figures in fits of uncontrollable sobbing. Politicians and managers cry when they apologise for committing a crime, the baseball team weep when they have lost a game and showgirls get all emotional remembering their childhoods. Not shedding tears at a friend's wedding or your offspring's graduation is tantamount to a lack of sincerity. In Japan, crying on certain occasions is not only socially acceptable but mandatory.

2

'Japan is the land of order.'

Tidiness, simplicity and muted elegance are the norms we associate with Japan, from the minimalism of a Zen garden to the transience of *wabi-sabi*. We picture football fans collecting rubbish from the stadium, schoolchildren washing the classroom floor and fresh flowers in public toilets. This sense of collective responsibility towards what is public is often countered by cramped and cluttered private homes. Mangas stacked up in the corridor, laundry hanging from curtain rails, supplies of tissues or bags of rice, pots and utensils standing precariously on kitchen surfaces. A family shares everything from bathwater to bedrooms but not household chores, which are still a mother's prerogative.

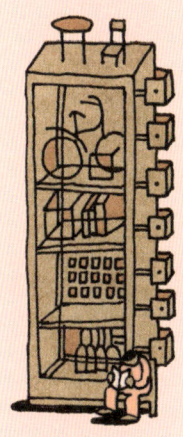

'Champions of politeness.'

3

Omotenashi ('hospitality') is the search for harmony through understanding a guest's needs. Using telephones on the bus is forbidden, sick people wear anti-contagion masks, taxi drivers ensure their passengers are comfortable and lost property is always returned. The more distant the connection to somebody, the more important it is to be polite. However, there are times when being *impolite* is a social expectation. In keeping with strict hierarchy, it is normal for a manager to assert himself forcefully with his staff, for a customer to talk down to a sales assistant and for a coach to be ruthless with his team. To be the object of *impoliteness* is confirmation that you truly belong to the group.

The Number

MATTEO BATTARRA
Translated by Katherine Gregor

It's funny – even bordering on the paradoxical – to think that the average age of the Japanese (forty-six, the highest in the world) should be almost twice that of their houses (twenty-seven, the lowest in the industrialised world). That's right: the average age of buildings in Tokyo and other Japanese cities is under thirty. This figure is surprising and difficult to associate with one of the richest countries on the planet, although it does explain political decisions and the way Japanese society has developed.

Such a short lifespan doesn't mean that most houses in Japan are poorly built. This is, essentially, an artificial 'use-by date'. Since the post-war period, in order to encourage and keep the building sector healthy, the Japanese government has been putting a lifespan limit of thirty years on all buildings: in practice, they calculated the average age of the houses that had to be knocked down or adapted to new anti-earthquake regulations to thirty years, so this figure became the national standard with which to comply (although, naturally, most public buildings and skyscrapers are built to last longer).

However, this 'law of impermanence' was not a revolutionary act so much as an acknowledgement that the country had, throughout most of its history, used timber as its principal building material and had to take into account the high risk of fires, especially in large cities where wooden houses and shops were packed close together. Tokyo, for one, has been repeatedly ravaged by terrible fires, as in 1657 and 1923, following the Great Kantō Earthquake. Moreover, this decision is closely connected with Japan's relationship with the preservation of its own past: the true historical and material worth of a building does not reside in the stones it is made of but rather its symbolic and geographical importance. A perfect illustration is the Ise Grand Shrine (the principal Shinto holy site), which is knocked down and rebuilt every twenty years. As in the case of other temples, this is the only way of making it really eternal and indestructible – and it is thanks to this process that craft techniques of building

27 years

The average age of the Japanese house

and working with wood can be preserved.

The results of this institutionalised tradition are manifold – some intentional, others involuntary. First and foremost, there is the development and prosperity of the building sector and seismic safety in cities. Second, there is the undoubtedly positive impact on the creativity of architects (such a limited life expectancy allows them more freedom to experiment with methods and ideas), so much so that Japanese architecture training has become a benchmark internationally. At the same time there have been profound effects on the way the property market operates: the value of a house is often lower than the land on which it has been built, so it is almost always cheaper to demolish and rebuild rather than to undertake the expense of a restoration and compliance with new standards. However, this apparently immutable process is now buckling under the weight of an ageing population. If, as demographers believe, by 2040 one-third of residents will be over sixty-five, clearly the demand for new houses will shrink. Moreover, there is the economic crisis. After decades of recession and stagnation, new generations are increasingly poorer than their parents and, partly through necessity and partly because they can, young Japanese are discovering the charm of buying old houses and fixing them up, while large building companies, such as Daiwa House, have spotted a business opportunity and are getting involved in the sector. So, after years of governments having a hand in breaking up traditional extended families and encouraging young people to follow the model of the American nuclear family in a terraced house, it is somewhat ironic that many town councils are currently contributing towards the reconstruction of the old social fabric by providing young couples with an incentive to refurbish their parents' houses and carry on living in the same district: 'No, it's not old, darling, it's "period".'

Ghosts of the Tsunami

Here and on pages 18–19: Tsunami defence walls along the coast of Tōhoku, Miyagi Prefecture; when the project is completed, these concrete seawalls, standing up to fourteen metres high, will extend along roughly four hundred kilometres of coastline.

The 2011 tsunami reinvigorated the ancestor cult, Japan's true religion. Survivors still report mysterious apparitions and disturbing cases of possession. The British writer Richard Lloyd Parry visits Reverend Kaneta, who provides them with spiritual assistance, listening to their stories and those of the suffering souls taking possession of their bodies.

RICHARD LLOYD PARRY

I met a priest in the north of Japan who exorcised the spirits of people who had drowned in the tsunami. The ghosts did not appear in large numbers until later in the year, but Reverend Kaneta's first case of possession came to him after less than a fortnight. He was chief priest at a Zen temple in the inland town of Kurihara. The earthquake on 11 March 2011 was the most violent that he or anyone he knew had ever experienced. The great wooden beams of the temple's halls had flexed and groaned with the strain. Power, water and telephone lines were fractured for days; deprived of electricity, people in Kurihara, fifty kilometres from the coast, had a dimmer idea of what was going on there than television viewers on the other side of the world. But it became clear enough when first a handful of families and then a mass of them began arriving at Kaneta's temple with corpses to bury.

Nearly twenty thousand people had died at a stroke. In the space of a month Kaneta performed funeral services for two hundred of them. More appalling than the scale of death was the spectacle of the bereaved survivors. 'They didn't cry,' Kaneta said to me a year later. 'There was no emotion at all. The loss was so profound, and death had come so suddenly. They understood the facts of their situation individually – that they had lost their homes, lost their livelihoods and lost their families. They understood each piece, but they couldn't see it as a whole, and they couldn't understand what they should do or sometimes even where they were. I couldn't really talk to them, to be honest. All I could do was stay with them and read the sutras and conduct the ceremonies. That was the thing I could do.'

Amid this numbness and horror, Kaneta received a visit from a man he knew, a local builder whom I will call Ono Takeshi. Ono was ashamed of what had happened and didn't want his real name to be published. 'He's such an innocent person,' Kaneta said to me. 'He takes everything at face value. You're from England, aren't you? He's like your Mr Bean.' I wouldn't have gone so far, because there was nothing ridiculous about Ono. He was a strong, stocky man in his late thirties, the kind of man most comfortable in blue overalls. But he had a dreamy ingenuousness that made the story he told all the more believable.

He had been at work on a house when the earthquake struck. He clung to the ground for as long as it lasted; even his lorry shook as if it was about to topple over. The drive home, along roads without traffic lights, was alarming, but the physical damage was remarkably slight: a few telegraph poles lolling at an angle, toppled garden walls. As the owner of a small building

Writer and journalist RICHARD LLOYD PARRY is the foreign correspondent for *The Times* based in Tokyo. He has written highly successful narrative non-fiction books on Indonesia, including *In the Time of Madness: Indonesia on the Edge of Chaos* (Jonathan Cape, 2005), and Japan; *People Who Eat Darkness* (Jonathan Cape, 2011) was the result of a ten-year investigation into the mysterious death of a young English woman in Tokyo, while *Ghosts of the Tsunami* (Jonathan Cape, 2017) deals with the subjects explored in this article.

firm, no one was better equipped to deal with the practical inconveniences inflicted by an earthquake. Ono spent the next few days busying himself with camping stoves, generators and jerry cans and paying little attention to the news.

But once television was restored it was impossible to be unaware of what had happened. Ono watched the endlessly replayed image of the explosive plume above the nuclear reactor, and the mobile-phone films of the black wave crunching up ports, houses, shopping centres, cars and human figures. These were places he had known all his life, fishing towns and beaches just over the hills, an hour's drive away. And watching their destruction produced in Ono a feeling common at that time, even among those most directly affected by displacement and bereavement. Although what had happened was undeniable – the destruction of entire towns and villages, the extinction of a multitude – it was also impossible. Impossible and, in fact, absurd. Insupportable, soul-crushing, unfathomable – but also just silly.

'My life had returned to normal,' he told me. 'I had fuel, I had an electricity generator, no one I knew was dead or hurt. I hadn't seen the tsunami myself, not with my own eyes, so I felt as if I was in a kind of dream.'

Ten days after the disaster Ono, his wife and his widowed mother drove over the mountains to see for themselves. They left in the morning in good spirits, stopped on the way to go shopping and reached the coast in time for lunch. For most of the journey the scene was familiar: brown rice fields, villages of wood and tile, bridges over wide slow rivers. Once they had climbed into the hills they passed more and more emergency vehicles, not only those of the police and fire services but military trucks of the Japan Self-Defense Forces. As the road descended towards the coast, their jaunty mood began to evaporate. Suddenly, before they understood where they were, they had entered the tsunami zone.

There was no advance warning, no marginal area of incremental damage. The wave had come in with full force, spent itself and stopped at a point as clearly defined as the reach of a high tide. Above it, nothing had been touched; below it, everything was changed.

No still photograph was capable of describing it. Even television images failed to encompass the panoramic quality of the disaster, the sense within the plain of destruction of being surrounded by it on all sides. In describing the landscapes of war we often speak of 'total' devastation. But even the most intense aerial bombing leaves walls and foundations of burned-out buildings as well as parks and woods, roads and tracks, fields and cemeteries. The tsunami spared nothing and achieved feats of surreal juxtaposition that no mere explosion could match. It plucked forests up by their roots and scattered them many kilometres inland. It peeled the macadam off the roads and cast it hither and thither in buckled ribbons. It stripped houses to their foundations and lifted cars, lorries, ships and corpses on to the tops of tall buildings.

At this point in Ono's narrative he became reluctant to describe in detail what he did or where he went. 'I saw the rubble, I saw the sea,' he said. 'I saw buildings damaged by the tsunami. It wasn't just the things themselves but the atmosphere. It was a place I used to go so often. It was such a shock to see it. And all the police and soldiers there. It's difficult to describe. It felt dangerous. My first feeling was that this is terrible. My next thought was: "Is it real?"'

Ono, his wife and his mother sat down for dinner as usual that evening. He remembered that he drank two small cans

> **'Ono's wife and mother described the events of the night before, after the round of needy phone calls. How he had jumped down on all fours and begun licking the tatami mats and futon and squirmed on them like a beast.'**

of beer with the meal. Afterwards, and for no obvious reason, he began calling friends on his phone. 'I'd just ring and say, "Hi, how are you?" – that kind of thing,' he told me. 'It wasn't that I had much to say. I don't know why, but I was starting to feel very lonely.'

His wife had already left the house when he woke the next morning. Ono had no particular work of his own and passed an idle day at home. His mother bustled in and out, but she seemed mysteriously upset, even angry. When his wife got back from her office she was similarly tense. 'Is something wrong?' Ono asked.

'I'm divorcing you!' she replied.

'Divorce? But why? Why?'

And so his wife and mother described the events of the night before, after the round of needy phone calls. How he had jumped down on all fours and begun licking the tatami mats and futon and squirmed on them like a beast. How at first they had nervously laughed at his tomfoolery but then been silenced when he began snarling, 'You must die. You must die. Everyone must die. Everything must die and be lost.' In front of the house was an unsown field, and Ono had run out into it and rolled over and over in the mud, as if he were being tumbled by a wave, shouting, 'There, over there! They're all over there – look!' Then he had stood up and walked out into the field, calling, 'I'm coming to you. I'm coming over to that side,' before his wife physically wrestled him back into the house. The writhing and bellowing went on all night until, around five in the morning, Ono cried out, 'There's something on top of me,' collapsed and fell asleep.

'My wife and my mother were so anxious and upset,' he said. 'Of course, I told them how sorry I was. But I had no memory of what I did or why.'

It went on for three nights. The next evening, as darkness fell, he saw figures walking past the house: parents and children, a group of young friends, a grandfather and a child. 'They were covered in mud,' he said. 'They were no more than five or six metres away, and they stared at me, but I wasn't afraid. I just thought, "Why are they in those muddy things? Why don't they change their clothes? Perhaps their washing machine's broken." They were like people I might have known once or seen before somewhere. The scene was flickering, like a film. But I felt perfectly normal, and I thought that they were just ordinary people.'

The next day Ono was lethargic and inert. At night he would lie down, sleep heavily for ten minutes, then wake up as lively and refreshed as if eight hours had passed. He staggered when he walked, glared at his wife and mother and even waved a knife. 'Drop dead!' he would snarl. 'Everyone else is dead, so die!'

After three days of pleading by his family he went to Reverend Kaneta at the temple. 'His eyes were dull,' Kaneta said. 'Like a person with depression after taking their medication. I knew at a glance that something was wrong.' Ono recounted the visit to the coast, and his wife and mother described his behaviour in the days since. 'The Reverend was looking hard at me as I spoke,' Ono said, 'and in part of my mind I was saying, "Don't look at me like that, you bastard. I hate your guts! Why are you looking at me?"'

Kaneta took Ono by the hand and led him into the main hall of the temple. 'He told me to sit down. I was not myself. I still remember that strong feeling of resistance. But part of me was also relieved – I wanted to be helped and to believe in the priest. The part of me that was still me wanted to be saved.'

Kaneta beat the temple drum as he chanted the Heart Sutra:

There are no eyes, no ears, no nose, no tongue, no body, mind; no colour, sound, or smell; no taste, no touch, no thing; no realm of sight, no realm of thoughts; no ignorance, no end to ignorance; no old age and no death; no end to age and death; no suffering, nor any cause of suffering, nor end to suffering, no path, no wisdom and no fulfilment.

Ono's wife told him that he pressed his hands together in prayer and that, as the priest's recitation continued, they rose high above his head as if being pulled from above. The priest splashed him with holy water, and then suddenly he returned to his senses and found himself with wet hair and shirt, filled with a sensation of tranquillity and release. 'My head was light,' he said. 'In a moment, the thing that had been there had gone. I felt fine physically, but my nose was blocked, as if I'd come down with a heavy cold.'

Kaneta spoke to him sternly; they both understood what had happened. 'Ono told me that he'd walked along the beach in that devastated area, eating an ice cream,' the priest said. 'He even put up a sign in the car in the windscreen saying "disaster relief" so that no one would stop him. He went there flippantly, without giving it any thought at all. I told him, "You fool. If you go to a place where many people have died, you must go with a feeling of respect. That's common sense. You have suffered a kind of punishment for what you did. Something got hold of you, perhaps the dead who cannot accept yet that they are dead. They have been trying to express their regret and their resentment through you."' Kaneta smiled as he remembered it. 'Mr Bean!' he said. 'He's so innocent and open. That's another reason they were able to possess him.'

Ono recognised all this, and more. It wasn't just the spirits of men and women that had possessed him, he saw now, but also animals – cats and dogs and other beasts which had drowned with their masters.

He thanked the priest and drove home. His nose was streaming as if with catarrh, but what came out was not mucus but a bright-pink jelly like nothing he had seen before.

*

The wave penetrated no more than a few kilometres inland, but over the hills in Kurihara it transformed the life of Reverend Kaneta. He had inherited his temple as the son and grandson of the previous priests, and the task of dealing with the survivors of the tsunami had tested him in ways for which he was unprepared. It had been the greatest disaster of post-war Japan: no larger single loss of life had occurred since the bombing of Nagasaki in 1945. And yet the pain did not announce itself; it dug underground and burrowed

TSUNAMI

On 11 March 2011, at 2.46 in the afternoon local time, a magnitude 8.9–9 earthquake hit the northeast coast of Japan in the Miyagi Prefecture. Its epicentre was in the sea, and a tsunami soon followed. The earth shook for six minutes in what was the most powerful earthquake ever measured in Japan and the fourth most powerful anywhere in the world. The island was shifted four metres to the east, and the damage caused is valued at US$210 billion, the most expensive natural disaster of all time. Japan had often seen similar events because of its location, but now it

was facing a catastrophe on a scale never previously seen. The tsunami generated waves up to forty metres high, which engulfed houses, streets, boats and people, with aftershocks that were felt thousands of kilometres away in different parts of the world. Two nuclear power stations, Fukushima Dai-ichi and Fukushima Dai-ni, were badly damaged, and several explosions and radiation leaks followed, leading to a state of nuclear emergency being declared, the first in Japan's history. Recent figures put the death toll from the disaster at 15,894 people with over 2,500 missing.

deep. Once the immediate emergency had abated, once the bodies were cremated, the memorial services held and the homeless sheltered, Kaneta set about trying to gain entry into the dungeon of silence in which he saw so many of the survivors languishing.

He began travelling around the coast with a group of fellow priests, organising an event he called Café de Monku – a bilingual pun: as well as being the Japanese pronunciation of the English word monk, *monku* means complaint. 'We think it will take a long time to get back to a calm, quiet, ordinary life,' the flyer said. 'Why don't you come and join us – take a break and have a little moan? The monks will listen to your complaint – and have a *monku* of their own, too.'

Under this pretext – a casual cup of tea and a friendly chat – people came to the temples and community centres where Café de Monku was held. Many lived in 'temporary residences', the grim prefabricated huts, freezing in winter and sweltering in summer, where those who could afford nothing better ended up. The priests listened sympathetically and made a point of not asking too many questions. 'People don't like to cry,' Kaneta said. 'They see it as selfish. Among those who are living in the temporary homes there's hardly anyone who hasn't lost a member of their family. Everyone's in the same boat, so they don't like to seem self-indulgent. But when they start talking, and when you listen to them and sense their gritted teeth and their suffering, all the suffering they can't and won't express, in time the tears come, and they flow without end.'

Haltingly, apologetically, then with increasing fluency, the survivors spoke of the terror of the wave, the pain of bereavement and their fears for the future. They also talked about encounters with the supernatural. They described sightings of ghostly strangers, friends and neighbours and dead loved ones. They reported hauntings at home, at work, in offices and public places, on the beaches and in the ruined towns. The experiences ranged from eerie dreams and feelings of vague unease to cases, like that of Takeshi Ono, of outright possession.

A young man complained of pressure on his chest at night, as if some creature was straddling him as he slept. A teenage girl spoke of a fearful figure who squatted in her house. A middle-aged man hated to go out in the rain because the eyes of the dead stared out at him from puddles.

A civil servant in Sōma visited a devastated stretch of coast and saw a solitary woman in a scarlet dress far from the nearest road or house, with no means of transport in sight. When he looked for her again she had disappeared.

A fire station in Tagajō received calls to places where all the houses had been destroyed by the tsunami. The crews went out to the ruins anyway and prayed for the spirits of those who had died – and the ghostly calls ceased.

A cab driver in the city of Sendai picked up a sad-faced man who asked to be taken to an address that no longer existed. Halfway through the journey he looked into his mirror to see that the rear seat was empty. He drove on anyway, stopped in front of the levelled foundations of a destroyed house and politely opened the door to allow the invisible passenger out at his former home.

At a refugee community in Onagawa, an old neighbour would appear in the living rooms of the temporary houses and sit down for a cup of tea with their startled occupants. No one had the heart to tell her that she was dead; the cushion on which she had sat was wet with seawater.

'When opinion polls put the question "How religious are you?" the Japanese rank among the most ungodly people in the world. It took a catastrophe for me to understand how misleading this self-assessment is.'

Priests – Christian and Shinto as well as Buddhist – found themselves called on repeatedly to quell unhappy spirits. A Buddhist monk wrote an article in a learned journal about 'the ghost problem', and academics at Tōhoku University began to catalogue the stories. 'So many people are having these experiences,' Kaneta told me. 'It's impossible to identify who and where they all are. But there are countless such people, and I think that their number is going to increase. And all we do is treat the symptoms.'

*

When opinion polls put the question 'How religious are you?' the Japanese rank among the most ungodly people in the world. It took a catastrophe for me to understand how misleading this self-assessment is. It is true that the organised religions, Buddhism and Shinto, have little influence on private or national life, but over the centuries both have been pressed into the service of the true faith of Japan: the cult of the ancestors.

I knew about the 'household altars', or *butsudan*, which are still seen in most homes and on which the memorial tablets of dead ancestors – the *ihai* – are displayed. The *butsudan* are black cabinets of lacquer and gilt, with openwork carvings of lions and birds; the *ihai* are upright tablets of black polished wood, vertically inscribed in gold. Offerings of flowers, incense, rice, fruit and drinks are placed before them; at the summer Festival of the Dead, families light candles and lanterns to welcome home the ancestral spirits. I had assumed that these picturesque practices were matters of symbolism and custom, attended to in the same way that people in the West will participate in a Christian funeral without any literal belief in the words of the liturgy. But in Japan spiritual beliefs are regarded less as expressions of faith than as simple common sense, so lightly and casually worn that it is easy to miss them altogether. 'The dead are not as dead there as they are in our own society,' the religious scholar Herman Ooms writes. 'It has always made perfect sense in Japan, as far back as history goes, to treat the dead as more alive than we do … even to the extent that death becomes a variant, not a negation of life.'

At the heart of ancestor worship is a contract. The food, drink, prayers and rituals offered by their descendants gratify the dead, who, in turn, bestow good fortune on the living. Families vary in how seriously they take these ceremonies, but, even for the unobservant, the dead play a continuing part in domestic life. For much of the time their status is something like that of beloved, deaf and slightly batty old folk who can't expect to be at the centre of the family but who are made to feel included on important occasions. Young people who have passed important entrance examinations, got a job or made a good marriage kneel before the *butsudan* to report their success. Victory or defeat in an important legal case, for example, will be shared with the ancestors in the same way.

Sotōba, wooden markers inscribed with texts from the sutras and the Buddhist name of the deceased; after the funeral ceremony the deceased is given a new name by the Buddhist priests.

When grief is raw the presence of the deceased is overwhelming. In households that lost children in the tsunami it became routine, after half an hour of tea and chat, to be asked if I would like to 'meet' the dead sons and daughters. I would be led to a shrine covered with framed photographs, toys, favourite drinks and snacks, letters, drawings and school exercise books. One mother had commissioned Photoshopped portraits of her children, showing them as they would have been had they lived: a boy who died in primary school smiling proudly in high-school uniform, a teenage girl as she should have looked in a kimono at her coming-of-age ceremony. Here, every morning, she began the day by talking to her dead children, weeping love and apology, as unselfconsciously as if she were speaking over a long-distance telephone line.

The tsunami did appalling violence to the religion of the ancestors. Along with walls, roofs and people, the water carried away household altars, memorial tablets and family photographs. Cemetery vaults were ripped open and the bones of the dead scattered. Temples were destroyed, along with memorial books listing the names of ancestors over generations. 'The memorial tablets – it's difficult to exaggerate their importance,' Taniyama Yōzō, a priest and friend of Reverend Kaneta, told me. 'When there's a fire or an earthquake, the *ihai* are the first thing many people will save, before money or documents. People died in the tsunami because they went home for the *ihai*. It's life – like saving your late father's life.'

When people die violently or prematurely, in anger or anguish, they are at risk of becoming *gaki*, 'hungry ghosts', who wander between worlds, propagating curses and mischief. There are rituals for placating unhappy spirits, but in the aftermath of the disaster few families were in a position to perform them. And then there were those ancestors whose descendants were entirely wiped out by the wave. Their comfort in the afterlife depended entirely on the reverence of living families, which had been permanently and irrevocably cut off: their situation was as helpless as that of orphaned children.

Thousands of spirits had passed from life to death; countless others were cut loose from their moorings in the afterlife. How could they all be cared for? Who was to honour the compact between the living and the dead? In such circumstances, how could there fail to be a swarm of ghosts?

*

Even before the tsunami struck its coast, nowhere in Japan was closer to the world of the dead than Tōhoku, the northern part of the island of Honshu. In ancient times it was a notorious frontier realm of barbarians, goblins and bitter cold. For modern Japanese it remains a remote, marginal, faintly melancholy place, of thick dialects and quaint conservatism, the symbol of a rural tradition that, for city dwellers, is no more than a folk memory. Tōhoku has bullet trains and smartphones and all the other 21st-century conveniences, but it also has secret Buddhist cults, a lively literature of supernatural tales and a sisterhood of blind shamanesses who gather once a year at a volcano called Osore-zan, or Mt Fear, the traditional entrance to the underworld.

Hijikata Masashi, the closest thing you could find to a Tōhoku nationalist, understood immediately that after the disaster hauntings would follow. 'We remembered the old ghost stories,' he said, 'and we told one another that there would be many new stories like that. Personally, I don't believe in the existence of spirits, but that's not

> **"'Some people are experiencing trauma," Hijikata explained, "and if your mental health is suffering then you need medical treatment. Others will rely on the power of religion. What we do is to create a place where people can accept the fact that they are witnessing the supernatural.'"**

the point. If people say they see ghosts, then that's fine – we can leave it at that.'

Hijikata was born in Hokkaido, Japan's northernmost island, but came to Sendai as a university student, and has the passion of the successful immigrant for his adopted home. When I met him he was running a small publishing company whose books and journals were exclusively on Tōhoku subjects. Prominent among his authors was the academic Akasaka Norio, a stern critic of the policies of the central government towards the region. These had been starkly illuminated by the nuclear disaster in Fukushima: an industrial plant erected by Tokyo, supplying electricity to the capital, and now spitting radiation over people who had enjoyed none of its benefits. 'Before the war it used to be said that Tōhoku provided men as soldiers, women as prostitutes and rice as tribute,' Akasaka wrote. 'I had thought that that kind of colonial situation had changed, but after the disaster I changed my thinking.'

Hijikata explained the politics of ghosts to me, as well as the opportunity and the risk they represented for the people of Tōhoku. 'We realised that so many people were having experiences like this,' he said, 'but there were people taking advantage of them. Trying to sell them this and that, telling them, "This will give you relief."' He met a woman who had lost her son in the disaster and who was troubled by a sense of being haunted. She went to the hospital: the doctor gave her anti-depressants. She went to the temple: the priest sold her an amulet and told her to read the sutras. 'But all she wanted,' he said, 'was to see her son again. There are so many like her. They don't care if they are ghosts – they want to encounter ghosts. Given all that, we thought we had to do something. Of course, there are some people who are experiencing trauma, and if your mental health is suffering then you need medical treatment. Other people will rely on the power of religion, and that is their choice. What we do is to create a place where people can accept the fact that they are witnessing the supernatural. We provide an alternative for helping people through the power of literature.'

Hijikata revived a literary form which had flourished in the feudal era: the *kaidan*, or 'weird tale'. *Kaidankai*, or 'weird tale parties', had been a popular summer pastime, when the delicious chill imparted by ghost stories served as a form of pre-industrial air conditioning. Hijikata's *kaidankai* were held in modern community centres and public halls. They would begin with a reading by one of his authors. Then members of the audience would share experiences of their own: students, housewives, working people, retirees. He organised *kaidan*-writing competitions and published the best of them in an anthology. Among the winners was Sutō Ayane, whom I met one afternoon at Hijikata's office.

She was a calm, neat young woman with black glasses and a fringe, who worked in Sendai at a care home for the disabled. The fishing port of Kesennuma, where she grew up, was one of the towns worst hit by the tsunami. Ayane's family home was beyond the reach of the wave, and her mother, sister and grandparents were untouched by it. But her father, a maritime engineer, worked in an office on the town's harbour front, and that evening he didn't come home.

'I thought about him all the time,' Ayane said. 'It was obvious something had happened. But I said to myself that he might just be injured – he might be lying in hospital somewhere. I knew that I should prepare for the worst. But I wasn't prepared at all.' She passed painful days in Sendai, trying to clear up the mess caused in her flat by the earthquake, thinking always of her father. Two weeks after the disaster, his body was found.

She arrived back at her family home just before the coffin was carried in. Friends and extended family had gathered, most of them casually dressed: everything black, everything formal, had been washed away. 'He hadn't drowned, as most people did,' Ayane said. 'He died of a blow to the chest from some big piece of rubble. In the coffin you could only see his face through a glass window. It had been a fortnight, and I was afraid that his body might have decayed. I looked through the window. I could see that he had a few cuts, and he was pale. But it was still the face of my father.' She wanted to touch his face for the last time, but the casket and its window had been sealed shut. On it lay a white flower, a single cut stem placed on the coffin's wood by the undertaker. There was nothing unusual about it. But to Ayane it was extraordinary. Ten days earlier, at the height of her hope and despair, in an effort to escape her anxiety, Ayane had gone to a big public bathhouse to soak in the hot spring water. When she came out she retrieved her boots from the locker and felt an obstruction in the toe as she pulled them on. 'I could feel how cold it was,' she remembered, 'even through my socks. And it felt soft, fluffy.' She reached in and removed a white flower, as fresh and flawless as if had just been cut.

A minor mystery: how could such an object have found its way into a boot inside a locked container? It faded from her mind, until that moment in front of her father's coffin, when the same flower presented itself again. 'The first time, I had the feeling that this might be a premonition of bad news,' Ayane said. 'Dad might not be alive any more, and this might be a sign of his death. But then I thought about it later, about the coolness of the flower, and the whiteness of the flower, and that feeling of softness against my toe. And I thought of that as the touch of my father, which I couldn't experience when he was in his coffin.'

Ayane knew that the flower was just a flower. She didn't believe in ghosts or that her dead father had sent it to her as a sign – if such communication was possible, why would a loving parent express it in such obscure terms? 'I think it was a coincidence,' she said, 'and that I made something good of it. When people see ghosts, they are telling a story, a story which has been broken off. They dream of ghosts because then the story carries on or comes to a conclusion. And if that brings them comfort, that's a good thing.'

Committed to print as a *kaidan*, published in Hijikata's magazine, it took on greater significance. 'There were thousands of deaths, each of them different,'

A shrine commemorating the victims in Hiyoriyama, Natori, Miyagi Prefecture, which was rebuilt in 2013 after being swept away by the waves in 2011.

> '"I asked, 'Who are you, and what do you want?'" he said. "When it spoke, it didn't sound like her at all. It talked for three hours." It was the spirit of a young woman whose mother had divorced and remarried and who found herself unloved and unwanted by her new family.'

Ayane said. 'Most of them have never been told. My father's name was Sutō Tsutomu. By writing about him, I share his death with others. Perhaps I save him in some way, and perhaps I save myself.'

*

I went back to see Reverend Kaneta in the late summer of 2013. Two and a half years had passed since the disaster, and inland there was no visible evidence of it at all. The towns and cities of Tōhoku were humming with the money being injected into the region for its reconstruction. A hundred thousand people still lived in prefabricated houses, but these upsetting places were tucked away out of sight of the casual visitor. None of the towns destroyed by the wave had been rebuilt, but they had been scoured of rubble. Coarse, tussocky grass had overgrown the coastal strip, and those ruins that were still visible looked more like neglected archaeological sites than places of continuing pain and despair.

I visited Kaneta in his temple and sat in the room where he received visitors. Lined up on the tatami were dozens of small clay statues, which would be handed out to the patrons of Café de Monku. They were representations of Jizō, the bodhisattva associated with kindness and mercy, who consoles the living and the dead.

In this room, Kaneta told me, he recently met a 25-year-old woman whom I will call Takahashi Rumiko. She had telephoned him in June in a state of incoherent distress. She talked of killing herself; she shouted about things entering her. That evening a car pulled up at the temple: Rumiko, her mother, sister and fiancé were inside. She was a nurse from Sendai – 'a very gentle person', Kaneta said, 'nothing peculiar or unusual about her at all'. Neither she nor her family had been hurt by the tsunami. But for weeks, her fiancé said, she had been complaining of something pushing into her from a place deep below, of dead presences 'pouring out' invisibly around her. Rumiko herself was slumped over the table. She stirred as Kaneta addressed the creature within her. 'I asked, "Who are you, and what do you want?"' he said. 'When it spoke, it didn't sound like her at all. It talked for three hours.'

It was the spirit of a young woman whose mother had divorced and remarried and who found herself unloved and unwanted by her new family. She ran away and found work in the *mizu shōbai*, or 'water trade', the night-time world of clubs, bars and prostitution. There she became more and more isolated and depressed and fell under the influence of a morbid and manipulative man. Unknown to her family, unmourned by anyone, she killed herself. Since then, not a stick of incense had been lit in her memory.

Kaneta asked the spirit, 'Will you come with me? Do you want me to lead you to the light?' He took her to the main hall of the temple, where he recited the sutra and sprinkled holy water. By the time the prayers were done, at half past one in the morning, Rumiko had returned to herself, and she and her family went home.

Three days later she was back. She complained of great pain in her left leg; once again, she had the sensation of being stalked by an alien presence. The effort of keeping out the intruder was exhausting. 'That was the strain, the feeling that made her suicidal,' Kaneta said. 'I told her, "Don't worry – just let it in."' Rumiko's posture and voice immediately stiffened and deepened; Kaneta found himself talking to a gruff man with a peremptory manner of speech, a sailor of the old Imperial Navy who had died in action during the Second World War after his left leg had been gravely injured by a shell.

The priest spoke soothingly to the old veteran: he prayed and chanted, the interloper departed, and Rumiko was calm. But all of this was just a prologue. 'All the people who came,' Kaneta said, 'and each one of the stories they told had some connection with water.'

*

Over the course of summer 2013, Reverend Kaneta exorcised twenty-five spirits from Takahashi Rumiko. They came and went at the rate of several a week. All of them, after the wartime sailor, were ghosts of the tsunami. For Kaneta, the days followed a relentless routine. The telephone call from Rumiko would come in the early evening; at nine o'clock her fiancé would pull up in front of the temple and carry her out of the car. As many as three spirits would appear in a single session. Kaneta talked to each personality in turn, sometimes over several hours; he established their circumstances, calmed their fears and politely but firmly enjoined them to follow him towards the light. Kaneta's wife would sit with Rumiko; sometimes other priests were present to join in with the prayers. In the early hours of the morning, Rumiko would be driven home. 'Each time she would feel better and go back to Sendai and go to work,' Kaneta told me. 'But then, after a few days, she'd be overwhelmed again.' Out among the living, surrounded by the city, she would become conscious of the dead, a thousand importunate spirits pressing in on her and trying to get inside.

One of the first was a middle-aged man who, speaking through Rumiko, despairingly called the name of his daughter.

'Kaori!' said the voice. 'Kaori! I have to get to Kaori. Where are you, Kaori? I have to get to the school, there's a tsunami coming.'

The man's daughter had been at her school by the sea when the earthquake struck. He had rushed out of work and driven along the coast road to pick her up, when the water had overtaken him. His agitation was intense; he was impatient and suspicious of Kaneta.

The voice asked, 'Am I alive or not?'

'No,' Kaneta said. 'You are dead.'

'And how many people died?' the voice asked.

'Twenty thousand people died.'

'Twenty thousand? So many?'

Later Kaneta asked him where he was.

'I'm at the bottom of the sea. It is very cold.'

'Come up from the sea to the world of light,' Kaneta said.

'But the light is so small,' the man replied. 'There are bodies all around me, and I can't reach it. And who are you anyway? Who are you to lead me to the world of light?'

The conversation went around and around for two hours. Eventually, Kaneta said, 'You are a father. You understand

ŌKAWA ELEMENTARY SCHOOL

Richard Lloyd Parry has followed the story of the victims and survivors of the tsunami closely, bringing them together in his book, *Ghosts of the Tsunami* (Jonathan Cape, 2017), which focuses on the story of Ōkawa Elementary School. The village of Ōkawa, in the Tōhoku region, sits on the banks of the Kitakami river, three kilometres from the Pacific Ocean. The school had 108 pupils. Of the seventy-eight children who were in school when the tsunami hit, seventy-four died. More than an hour passed between the earthquake and the arrival of the tsunami, and the building was close to a hill that could have sheltered them and saved their lives. Witnesses said that the evacuation of the school had been carried out impeccably: within five minutes everyone was outside in the playground. What happened in that fateful hour between half past two and half past three? It transpired that, incredibly, the evacuation manual did not specify where people should go and take refuge in this kind of emergency. The teachers argued about what to do, and there was a general state of confusion. Some of the children wanted to go towards the hill but were stopped and told that the ground might give way. The situation was further complicated when other people living in the village turned up in the playground, which was listed in some resources as an assembly point in an emergency. After an investigation and a trial, the parents of the young victims obtained compensation from the authorities for the disastrous management of the emergency.

Pages 30–1: The shrine at Hiyoriyama, Natori, Miyagi Prefecture.

the anxieties of a parent. Consider this girl whose body you have used. She has a father and mother who are worried about her. Have you thought of that?'

There was a long pause, and the man said, 'You're right,' then moaned. Kaneta chanted the sutra. He paused from time to time when the voice uttered choked sounds, but they faded to mumbles and finally the man was gone.

Day after day, week after week, the spirits kept coming: men and women, young people and old, with accents rough and polished. They told their stories at length, but there was never enough specific detail – surnames, place names, addresses – to verify any individual account, and Kaneta felt no urge to. One man had survived the tsunami but killed himself after learning of the death of his two daughters. Another wanted to join the rest of his ancestors but couldn't find his way because his home and everything in it had been washed away. There was an old man who spoke in thick Tōhoku dialect. He was desperately worried about his wife, who had survived and was living alone and uncared-for in one of the bleak metal huts. In a shoebox she kept a white rope which she would contemplate and caress. He feared what she planned to use it for.

Kaneta reasoned and cajoled, prayed and chanted, and in the end each of the spirits gave way. But days or hours after one group of ghosts had been dismissed, more would stumble forward to take their

THE LANTERN FESTIVAL

Every year in Japan from 13 to 16 August people celebrate the ancient Buddhist festival of Obon, the festival of lanterns and also of the dead. It's a very important time when families clean and decorate their houses, dance and celebrate to welcome the souls of the dead who, it is believed, come back to their earthly home during the festival. City-dwelling Japanese often take a few days' holiday and return to their home towns and villages during this time. Families visit the graves of their dead relatives and offer generous gifts of food at the temples and altars found all around the country. In recent years the practice of releasing candle-lit paper lanterns into rivers and letting them float away with the current (*tōrō nagashi*) has become increasingly popular; it is said that the floating lanterns guide the spirits on their journey back to the afterlife once the festival is over.

place. One night in the temple, Rumiko announced, 'There are dogs all around me, it's loud! They are barking so loudly I can't bear it.' Then she said, 'No! I don't want it. I don't want to be a dog.' Finally she said, 'Give it rice and water to eat. I'm going to let it in.'

'She told us to seize hold of her,' Kaneta said, 'and when the dog entered her it had tremendous power. There were three men holding on to her, but they were not strong enough, and she threw them off. She was scratching the floor and roaring, a deep growl.' Later, after the chanting of the sutra and the return to her peaceful self, Rumiko recounted the story of the dog. It had been the pet of an old couple who lived close to the Fukushima Dai-ichi nuclear power plant. When the radiation began to leak, its owners had fled in panic with all their neighbours. But they forgot to unchain the dog, which slowly died of thirst and hunger. Later, when it was much too late, the spirit of the animal observed men in white protective suits coming in and peering at its shrivelled corpse.

In time, Rumiko became able to exercise control over the spirits; she spoke of a container, which she could choose to open or close. A friend of Kaneta, who was present at one of the exorcisms, compared her to a chronically ill patient habituated to vomiting: what at first was disgusting became over time familiar and bearable. By August she reported being able to brush the spirits away when they approached her. She was still conscious of their presence; they were no longer shoving and jostling her but skulking at the room's edge. The evening telephone calls and late-night visits became less and less frequent. Rumiko and her fiancé married and moved away from Sendai, and to his extreme relief Kaneta stopped hearing from her.

The effort of the exorcisms was too much. Friends were beginning to worry about him. 'I was overwhelmed,' he said. 'Over the months I'd become accustomed to hearing the stories of survivors. But all of a sudden I found myself listening to the voices of the dead.'

Most difficult to bear were the occasions when Rumiko was possessed by the personalities of children. 'When a child appeared,' Kaneta said, 'my wife took her hand. She said, "It's Mummy – it's Mummy here. It's all right, it's all right. Let's go together."' The first to appear was a tiny nameless boy, too young to understand what was being said to him or to do anything more than call for his mother over and over again. The second was a girl of seven or eight. She had been with her even younger brother when the tsunami struck and tried to run away with him. But in the water, as they were both drowning, she had let go of his hand; now she was afraid that her mother would be angry. 'There's a black wave coming,' she said. 'I'm scared, Mummy. Mummy, I'm sorry, I'm sorry.'

The voice of the girl was terrified and confused. Her body was drifting helplessly in the cold water, and it was a long struggle to guide her upwards towards the light. 'She gripped my wife's hand tightly until she finally came to the gate of the world of light,' Kaneta recalled. 'Then she said, "Mum, I can go on my own now, you can let go."'

Afterwards Mrs Kaneta tried to describe the moment when she released the hand of the young-woman-as-little-drowned-girl. The priest himself was weeping for her and for the twenty thousand other stories of terror and extinction. But his wife was aware only of a huge energy dissipating. It made her remember the experience of childbirth and the sense of power discharging at the end of pain as the newborn child finally enters the world.

The 'Do-It-Yourself' Women

For decades following the Second World War women's work was confined to the home, where they sewed, cooked, created and produced all manner of things. Having liberated themselves from the role of housewife and entering the world of work, many women are now dreaming – in these times of economic crisis, stress and fewer career prospects – of a return to the tranquil profession of 'domestic designer'.

SEKIGUCHI RYŌKO
Translated by Meredith McKinney

A vintage Shōwa-era advertisement in a street in Tokyo's Minowabashi district; Shōwa is the name given to the period of the reign of the Emperor Hirohito, 1926–89.

Looking back, it seems to me that women in post-war Japan were forever making things. It wasn't the same as the wartime women who were forced by necessity to make their own household tools and work in the fields; these post-war women with their ceaselessly active hands were 'beautifying' their lives by sewing things, making sweets for their children, planting flowers in their gardens, knitting sweaters for their husbands.

My mother was born in 1945, placing her fair and square in the second generation of post-war women who made things. In the early days she went off to work in an office dressed in skirts that her mother (my grandmother) had made for her – those skirts were, in turn, handed down to me, and I wore them as a high-school student. She'd stop off on the way home to attend flower-arranging lessons, and in due course she got a licence to teach the subject herself. In early summer she helped her mother dry plums for pickling. Later, when I was born, she embroidered my first baby clothes. When I went off to nursery school each day I carried a homemade lunch, then, when I came home, she'd devise homework tasks (replete with illustrations) to entertain me till supper time, a separate meal from the one she made for my father.

Perhaps when I went to primary school she found time heavy on her hands, for she started learning basket-weaving. She must have been dexterous; she tirelessly turned out baskets and containers then progressed to making bigger things such as woven chests of drawers – and eventually she started teaching a private basket-making class of her own.

I think that in the 1970s many of the women who were full-time housewives (the great majority of women back then) went to classes like these. Paper creations, doll-making, knitting, Western-style sewing ... these women had considerably more leisure than their mothers had had, and they threw themselves into hobbies that involved making things to decorate their homes and prettify their lives. I remember as a child often seeing in friends' houses patchwork bed quilts, Japanese dolls in glass cases on top of the piano, lacework telephone covers and toilet-paper-holder covers, all made by hand.

Later, the praise my mother received for the handmade sweets she would set out for her students after the lesson led her to offer cooking classes as well. This was in the late 1970s. It was probably also fortunate that we lived in a housing complex among a host of other families of roughly the same generation and income level. For a household in which the parents were in their late thirties, freshly burdened with loans for the home they'd purchased and with children of primary-school age, my mother's cooking skills must have been a useful way to offset expenditures and increase the opportunities for family time. I often called in on my way home from school to visit my mother in the local assembly hall that she rented for the various classes she taught most days, and I was plied with snacks and so forth – probably also a way of ameliorating a little the somewhat suffocating air of the housing complex and bringing private and public spaces enjoyably together.

Later we moved for my father's work, and my mother gave up teaching the

SEKIGUCHI RYŌKO is a poet and translator. She has lived in Paris since 1997 and writes in French as well as Japanese, often on food and culinary culture. She has been awarded the title of Chevalier de l'Ordre des Arts et Lettres in France.

> 'The young women were full of dreams about their future married life and the older ones confronted by the reality of a life shared with in-laws and other relatives.'

classes. Instead of living in the housing complex, we now found ourselves in a newly built detached house with a garden, close to Tokyo in the Shōnan area famous for its beach frontage. It was an upmarket place that ought to have delighted the wife of a company worker. But I observed how glumly my mother passed her days there. She knew no one in this new world, and there was no possibility of finding a place that would employ a housewife in her forties who had barely ever been out to work. It was surely a sense of female solidarity that helped me to realise how painful it was for my mother to find her life as an individual slipping from her grasp, for all that she had a life as wife and mother. My brother saw her role simply as that of mother, but I saw in her a version of the life I myself would no doubt have to live as a woman.

I don't remember very well how it came about, but some time later my mother's natural sociability led to her starting up a new cooking class. At first she held private lessons in her own home. Most of her students were soon-to-married young women in their twenties and married women in their thirties who wanted to keep learning. After the lesson was over they would stay on to drink tea and chat, and occasionally I joined in. The talk I heard among these two groups of women – the young ones full of dreams about their future married life and the older ones confronted by the reality of a life shared with in-laws and other relatives – provided a real 'women's education' for the teenage girl I then was.

My mother soon expanded her activities, travelling to teach, opening a café and making the menus for the trendy B&B-style *penshon* (pensions) that were then all the rage in Japan. The 1980s were the prosperous days of Japan's so-called bubble economy. My mother made special-order wedding cakes for couples wanting their own unique style of wedding, did the catering for the opening parties of gallery exhibitions and in general took on a wide variety of extravagant orders that sprang from the affluence of Japanese society at the time.

My father watched all this with some bitterness. No doubt he wasn't keen on this energetic activity in the wife he did love after a fashion. There are still things I don't understand about it even today. If he found her writing recipes or preparing for lessons he would shout, 'Quit that job of yours if you can't be a proper housewife!'

The symbolic halt to her independent activities finally came, I think, when she received a request from a cookery magazine to write a recipe column. My father came up with every reason he could think of as to why she shouldn't take it on. The money wasn't really the problem; I think what he didn't like was the thought of her name in print. (He also became extremely cross when I first won a literary award, berating and even at one point striking me, but that's another story.) My mother was up for doing the column at first, but he rejected the offer, declaring that if some child ate her food and anything untoward occurred then she'd be held responsible (the planned recipes were for weaning babies). On the surface my mother didn't seem particularly upset at having to relinquish her plan of writing recipes for the public, but it seems to me now that deep down this is the moment when she gave up all hope of building a career for herself in the cookery world and instead accepted the passive role of a woman dependent on her husband.

The nature of Japan's social-support system also presented a problem. The tax system stipulates that, whether wife or husband, the partner who doesn't work is classed as a 'dependent family member'. Once you earn more than ¥1,200,000 (c. US$11,000 or £8,500) a year you can no longer claim dependent status and have to pay tax independently, a disadvantage that means most women will work only part-time at best and keep their income below this limit. I think my mother could have earned enough to make it profitable even if she were forced to pay her own tax, but, faced with my father's opposition, she chose to limit her earnings to dependent levels. There was no way around it, she decided, and to me she presented an argument intended to convince herself, that she was at least lucky her husband was understanding about the work she did do.

But I simply couldn't see it that way. Why should a grown-up like her always have to bow to someone else's opinion simply because they were husband and wife? Surely he was also obliged, in that case, to listen to her? It was no doubt in order to convince herself that she had actively chosen to accept the constraints of the time – according to which it was a privilege to fulfil the role of wife – that, rather than simply caving in to this absurdity she pressured me into taking up cooking myself. My brother was exempt from such labours, but apparently, as a woman, I needed at least to master the kitchen so I could get married. Cooking, which involved the double bind of being both the means by which she might have become self-supportive and an activity limited to the home, thus became for her the kernel of a distorted kind of self-identity. For my mother, one judged people (specifically women) according to whether they could or couldn't cook, and for this reason I loathed cooking for many years. I couldn't accept an attitude that chose to reproduce for one's own children the social and marital constraints under which one was forced to live instead of attempting to reform them. It was then, I think, that a strong conviction that I must live a life of economic and social independence took hold of me.

In the 1990s a different type of student began to attend my mother's cooking lessons. There were increasing calls for her to run classes for middle-aged men who had never so much as set foot in a kitchen. This was a time when we were suddenly hearing the expression 'middle-age divorce' on everyone's lips. Men who had spent their lives working, whose role in the family had simply been to bring home the monthly salary, were suddenly retired and hanging about the home day in day out, and their wives couldn't stand it. The husband could do nothing in the way of housework and naturally took it for granted that his wife was the one to produce three meals a day for him, while from her point of view she was no longer free of the need to 'child-mind' her husband all day. No wonder their life together ran into problems. And so, to stave off the possibility of being served divorce papers (or sometimes on the orders of their wives), men in their fifties were heading off to beginners' cooking classes to learn how at least to cook the rice and the miso soup.

Workplace equality was still a long way off – much as it remains today, for that matter – and most people married in their twenties, but, in the private sphere at least,

Above: A poster from the Shōwa era.
Below: Hairnets in the market in Sugamo, a shopping district favoured by women over sixty.

Above: A scene from one of the films in the popular series of around forty movies (1969–95) starring the character Tora-san in the museum devoted to him in Shimabata, Tokyo.
Below: A flower arrangement at a sake distillery.
Page 42: A poster for a distillery along with ceramic bottles and drinking cups in an *izakaya*.

> 'In any society in which men fill most of the jobs, the possibilities for women to have any kind of career have always been intimately related to everyday life.'

small steps were being made towards some kind of equality of gender roles.

There were men around me who could cook, and I can remember my brother making sweets to take to the girl he was dating. This, I think, was what lay behind the shift in types of student at my mother's cooking classes. Take, for instance, the serialised manga *Cooking Papa*, launched in 1985 and still going today. Early in the series the protagonist Papa hid the fact that he liked cooking from his work colleagues, but in the late 1990s he started opening up to them about his role as Cooking Papa in the home.

In 1980 there were very few households in which both partners had full-time work, but this gradually shifted until in 1995 there were roughly equal numbers of women identifying as 'professional housewife' and households in which both partners were employed. At the same time another change was taking place. Much as not only cooking but making things in general had for my mother been a means of achieving autonomy, so now women were beginning to treat what they learned not simply as hobbies but as a first step in acquiring a skill they could later go on to teach. In the 1990s one often heard of women who had no sooner begun learning something than they were asking when they'd be able to start running their own courses in it – women who, no doubt, could neither return to their former jobs nor find interesting new work now that their child-rearing days were over and who were desperately looking around for some means of 'self-realisation'. This expression, so popular at the time, would surely not have been necessary if society had provided women with a firm foundation for returning to work. Women would have worked hard and suffered the usual ups and downs in their efforts at promotion, just as men do, but they would have had no need to cling to such vapid concepts as 'self-realisation'.

In any society in which men fill most of the jobs, the possibilities for women to have any kind of career have always centred on the sort of work that can be done at home by hand, work intimately related to everyday life such as sewing or cooking. But Japan was unusual in that, although it was neither a poor country (where, of course, even men can often not find work) nor a developing nation, for a long time women's work was artificially limited to the realm of the do-it-yourself. At a time when it was not unusual in the West for women to be in managerial positions, to be politicians, doctors, lawyers and so forth (and despite the fact that the Japanese believed they had caught up with and joined the West), in Japan women were still devotedly kneading bread, creating flower arrangements or making jelly as a substitute for the careers from which they were barred. Behind these apparently charming handmade creations lurked the dark reality of a society in which it was difficult for a woman to manage even the straightforward achievement of constructing a life for herself as an individual.

So what of today then? The number of couples in which both partners work has more than doubled since the days of the

COOKING PAPA

Cooking Papa is the original incarnation of the Cooking Manga genre (part of the *seinen* type of manga, which is aimed at an adult male audience but is not erotic), and it has been drawn without interruption by Ueyama Tochi ever since 1989. The protagonist, Araiwa Kazumi, is the classic salaryman (see page 174): hard working, stoical and tough. His wife Nijiko is a journalist and has little time to spend on domestic work, but, luckily, in this model family the father steps in: he's a good father, an exemplary boss and above all – especially given that *Cooking Papa* is a manga about the pleasures of food – an excellent cook, whose food delights those who eat it. Since 2008 the Manga Museum in Kyoto has regularly invited Ueyama Tochi to demonstrate some of the recipes from the manga in front of an audience at the museum and in 2017 it devoted a large retrospective exhibition to this cult series.

'professional wife' – but now many young women are apparently declaring that they want to be full-time housewives. It seems they would prefer to spend their days at home with their children rather than wear down their spirits through long days being forced to work in companies that offer no hope of a real career. No doubt there's also the added factor that, in these times when it's accepted that both will work, to be able to stay at home implies that you've caught yourself a high-earning husband who can support you.

Do these women not understand the bitterness nursed by the women of an earlier time as their hands worked at those charming creations? Evidently not. Looking at websites you find that women's handmade crafts are still out there on offer everywhere. All these women want to become 'creators'. It would seem that it's not so much an effect of the frustration they feel at being unable to advance socially or put their talents to good use so much as a loss of any faith they may have had in the Japanese workplace per se and the resulting urge to create startups of sorts for themselves by making things. You might think there would be other areas they could turn to for startup ideas, but no doubt handmade crafts are a compelling choice for anyone wanting to be able to work from home.

Perhaps, after all, this is a means for women to achieve autonomy and freedom today. Or perhaps in today's Japan, where the possibilities for other forms of 'self-realisation' are extremely limited, this is one small area that can offer a form of security.

Perhaps the do-it-yourself women will always be with us.

GENDER WAGE GAP

The gender wage gap is defined as the difference between median earnings of men and women relative to median earnings of men.
Gross earnings, decile ratios (%, 2018 or latest)

TOP 10

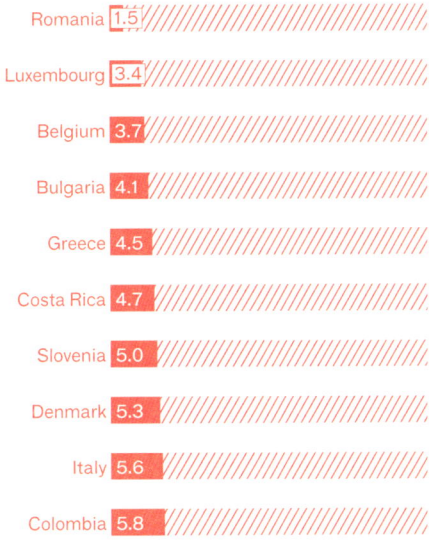

Romania	1.5
Luxembourg	3.4
Belgium	3.7
Bulgaria	4.1
Greece	4.5
Costa Rica	4.7
Slovenia	5.0
Denmark	5.3
Italy	5.6
Colombia	5.8

BOTTOM 10

Korea	34.6
Estonia	28.3
Japan	24.5
Israel	21.8
Latvia	21.1
EU	19.1
Canada	18.2
USA	18.2
Finland	17.7
UK	16.4

SOURCE: OECD

The (No Longer So) Secret Cult that Governs Japan

A Shinto sect following a monarchist, patriotic and revisionist programme – with a membership that includes Prime Minister Abe Shinzō and other prominent politicians – operates in the shadows of political power. It promotes the adoption of Shinto as Japan's state religion and is pushing for amendments to the country's pacifist constitution, including the abolition of Article 9, which forbids Japan from engaging in warfare as a means of settling international disputes.

JAKE ADELSTEIN

A man in military uniform takes part in the 15 August commemoration of the end of the Second World War at the Yasukuni Shrine; the shrine in central Tokyo is dedicated to the souls of the soldiers (including a number of war criminals) who died fighting in the emperor's service.

In the Land of the Rising Sun a conservative Shinto cult dating back to the 1970s – which includes Prime Minister Abe Shinzō and many of his cabinet among its adherents – was finally dragged out of the shadows in 2016. With Abe now in his third consecutive term (fourth in total) as prime minister, and now the longest serving prime minister in Japanese history, they may have come much closer to achieving their goals: a return to an imperial Japanese constitution and the abandonment of 'basic human rights, popular sovereignty and pacifism'.

The group is called Nippon Kaigi (Japan Conference) and is ostensibly run by Takubo Tadae, a former journalist turned political scientist. It has only thirty-eight thousand members, but like many an exclusive club or sect it wields tremendous political influence.

Shinto is a polytheistic and animist religion native to Japan. The state-sponsored Shintoism promulgated in the country before and during the Second World War also elevated the emperor to the status of a god and insisted that the Japanese – the Yamato – were a divine race and all other races inferior. Nippon Kaigi originated in the early 1970s as an offshoot of a liberal Shinto organisation known as Seichō no Ie. In 1974 a splinter group joined forces with Nippon wo Mamoru Kai, a state-Shinto-revival organisation that espoused patriotism and a return to emperor worship. The group in its current state was officially formed in May 1997, when Nippon wo Mamoru Kai and a group of right-leaning intellectuals joined forces. The current cult's goals are to gut Japan's post-war pacifist constitution, end sexual equality, get rid of foreigners, void pesky 'human rights' laws and return Japan to its imperial glory.

Prime Minister Abe has repeatedly expressed his ambition to proceed with reform of Japan's modern democratic constitution, which has remained sacred and inviolate since 1947, and the cult could soon have the opportunity to completely dominate the politics of the country, which could see a step back to the Meiji era (1868–1912) that ended more than a century ago. Then the emperor was supreme and freedom of expression subservient to the interests of the state.

Abe, a third-generation politician, is the grandson of Kishi Nobusuke, who was Japan's minister of munitions during the Second World War and arrested as a war criminal in 1945 before becoming prime minister in the 1950s. Abe is a staunch nationalist and historical revisionist who, prior to his current run as premier, also served as prime minister between 2006 and 2007 before resigning abruptly mid-term. His ties to Nippon Kaigi go back to the 1990s.

In line with fellow members of this imperial and imperialist cult, Abe has said the revision of the constitution is his

JAKE ADELSTEIN is a thoroughbred investigative journalist specialising in crime. He was born in Missouri but has lived much of his life in Japan and has been a long-standing writer for the country's leading newspaper, the *Yomiuri Shimbun*, as well as other publications. He told the story of his life as a reporter under threat from the yakuza in his book *Tokyo Vice: An American Reporter on the Police Beat in Japan* (Pantheon Books, 2009).

lifetime goal. In an interview in *Nikkei Asian Review*, published in February 2014, he stated: 'My party, the Liberal Democratic Party [LDP], has been advocating amending our constitution since its foundation almost sixty years ago.' And now Abe and his party, at least the extremist wing, are racing to achieve that goal while the public is distracted by the prospect of the 2020 Olympics.

Japan's parliament, the Kokkai, or Diet, is composed of an upper and lower house. Article 96 of the constitution stipulates that amendments can be made to the constitution if approved by a supermajority of two-thirds of both houses of the Diet and by simple majority in a referendum. At present the LDP and its coalition partners have a two-thirds majority in the Lower House and a simple majority in the Upper House.

While constitutional reform has always been the grand prize sought by the Abe administration, to the West and Japan it has always insisted that 'it's all about Abenomics', the economic policy designed to revitalise Japan's long-stagnant economy that Prime Minister Abe promised to put into action in 2012 (see page 53). It is based upon the 'three arrows' of fiscal stimulus, quantitative easing and structural reforms. The third 'arrow' has yet to be fired, and in 2016 the International Monetary Fund essentially declared Abenomics a failure and suggested Japan raise wages.

The LDP has put an internal ban on public statements about constitutional reform. This is savvy, notes Nakano Kōichi, a professor and expert on Japanese politics at Sophia University, Tokyo. 'Abenomics was simply a way of repackaging Abe's nationalism as something sexy so he could return to power.' He notes that public opinion is opposed by a large margin to the revision of the constitution. 'Abe, since 2012, has emphasised his economic platform and then proceeded to do what he intended to do once the election is over. He did this with the passing of the State Secrets Laws and then with the strongly opposed Security Laws in 2015 after the December 2014 snap elections. Perhaps he is getting advice from his deputy prime minister, who once remarked that the LDP should learn from the Nazis about how to quietly change a constitution.

The former leader of the Democratic Party of Japan, Okada Katsuya, has warned: 'Under the Abe administration basic human rights such as freedom of speech and the public's right to free access to information [about their government] have been threatened … the pacifism of the constitution will be destroyed.'

The LDP's original proposed constitution, which has been strongly influenced by Nippon Kaigi alumni, according to reports by the *Asahi Shimbun* and other media, would scrap Article 9, which forbids Japan from engaging in warfare as a means of settling international disputes. It would also severely curtail freedom of speech, taking away the right to speak out on issues 'if it is against the public interest'. Presumably, the government would decide what is 'the public interest'. It eliminates the words 'basic human rights' from key sections, as constitutional experts have noted. The LDP argues that revision is necessary for a modern Japan to deal with the threat of China and break free from 'the post-war regime'. Abe is currently suggesting only a watered-down version of Article 9 in his proposed constitutional reforms, but the original LDP blueprint has not been abandoned.

Up to 2016 the ideology that Prime Minister Abe and his colleagues espouse had received only modest scrutiny from Japan's mainstream media, but all that began to change with the publication of the surprise bestseller *Nippon kaigi no kenkyū* ('Research into Japan Conference') by former white-collar worker turned journalist Sugano Tamotsu. Then, Japan's leading constitutional expert, Kobayashi Setsu, who is a former member of Nippon Kaigi, said of the group that they 'have trouble accepting the reality that Japan lost the war' and wish to restore the Meiji-era constitution. Some members are descendants of the people who started the war, he notes. Kobayashi is so vexed by his former brethren that he created a new political party to promote and protect constitutional rights called, somewhat amusingly, Kokumin Ikari-no Koe (the Angry Voice of the People). To Nippon Kaigi he is a traitor and a nightmare; for Prime Minister Abe he is an angry, loud-mouthed headache.

Seichō no Ie, the spiritual forebear of Nippon Kaigi, has turned its back on the LDP and the ruling coalition as well – its first overt political act in decades. The organisation told the *Weekly Post* in 2016: 'The Abe government thinks lightly of the constitution, and we are opposed to their attempts to change Article 9. In addition, we feel distrust at their failure to uphold policy determined by law.'

Despite Nippon Kaigi's small numbers, half of the Abe cabinet belongs to the Nippon Kaigi National Lawmakers Friendship Association, the group's political offshoot. Prime Minister Abe himself is the special advisor. The former defence minister, Koike Yuriko, who became Tokyo's first female governor in 2016, is a prominent member. She is also a historical revisionist, tacitly denying that thousands of Koreans were slaughtered by Japanese mobs in 1923 and demanding that voting rights for Japan's resident foreigners be opposed. She has exhibited a streak of xenophobia and revisionism that is troubling.

AN EXCEPTIONAL REPORTER

Jake Adelstein, the author of this article, has attained almost mythical status over the years as a crime reporter with a relentless approach who will do anything for a story. *The New Yorker* added to this myth when it published a dramatic article about Adelstein in 2012 entitled 'All Due Respect', portraying him as a character from a detective story. His most famous investigation was into the yakuza boss Gotō Tadamasa, the pact Gotō made with the FBI to jump the queue for a liver transplant in the USA and the organ trafficking in which the yakuza were involved. Adelstein had to have bodyguards for many years because of threats from the Gotō clan in Japan, as did his family in the USA. Some critics have suggested that Adelstein went too far in his investigations, and that this was why he stopped working for the *Yomiuri Shimbun* newspaper, but there have also been rumours of links to the CIA. Over the years Adelstein became addicted to the adrenaline rush of dangerous investigations, and, according to the article in *The New Yorker*, he can't leave behind the role of the *homme fatal* of the Tokyo underworld, frequenting criminal circles in search of the next scoop. Those who know him insist that he is a man of his word, a characteristic highly prized in Japan: that might explain why he is still alive.

Above: A far-right group in uniform holding a Japanese flag take part in the celebrations at the Yasukuni Shrine to the war dead in Tokyo.
Below: The *gaisensha* (propaganda van) belonging to another group parked outside the shrine.

> 'Nippon Kaigi, he found, used *neto-uyo* (cyber right wingers who troll anyone on the internet they feel writes negatively about Japan), intellectuals, politicians and closet sympathisers in mainstream media to exert considerable influence on policy and public opinion.'

Sankei Shimbun and others have reported that Nippon Kaigi even tried to pressure the publisher Fusōsha into dropping Sugano's book. The protest letter sent to the publisher was, surprisingly, in the name of the group's secretary general, Kabushima Yūzo, not in the name of the chairman, Takubo Tadae. Kabushima is a staunch emperor worshipper and was a key member of Seichō no Ie's student movement. Sugano argues in his book that it is Kabushima who is really running the organisation. Despite the threatening tone of the letter, however, the publisher didn't budge. Originally, only eight thousand copies were printed; it has now sold over two hundred thousand. At least seven other books have been published on the group to date; magazines are running front-page stories about them.

Nippon Kaigi has become very visible.

Sugano was surprised and relieved to see Nippon Kaigi and its influence on national policy finally getting attention. He himself is a political conservative who graduated from the University of Texas with a degree in political science before returning to Japan over a decade ago. While he was living in Texas, where he picked up a bit of an accent, he noticed how the Christian evangelical movement exerted political influence and sees some parallels in their methods and those of Nippon Kaigi. Sugano was still a white-collar worker, a salaryman, when he first became aware of the existence of the group. Back in 2008 Sugano recalls the shift he felt in the atmosphere on the streets. 'Crazy people were starting to speak out,' he says. Protests led by groups such as the anti-foreigner hate-speech group Zaitokukai were more noticeable. He saw an ugly escalation of their activities with each passing day.

He found these hate-speech movements concerning and started to infiltrate their protests, documenting the events with photos and recordings. In order to understand the motives of members and supporters, he began to dig into the conservative publications often referenced in their online comments. The contributors who wrote for these publications puzzled him. Many were established in their field, journalists and academics, all contributing on topics unrelated to their expertise. This peculiar pattern helped him connect the dots: they all seemed to be members of one group. That realisation led him down the rabbit hole where he encountered the revisionist wonderland that is Nippon Kaigi.

Nippon Kaigi, he found, used *neto-uyo* (cyber right wingers who troll anyone on the internet they feel writes negatively about Japan), intellectuals, politicians and closet sympathisers in mainstream media to exert considerable influence on policy and public opinion. This included getting the Japanese government to reinstate the imperial calendar, which was banned by the Allied occupation government (1945–52). If it's 2020 in the West, under the imperial calendar, which is based on the reign of the current emperor (who ascended the

ONE PARTY, ONE EMPEROR

Japan is a constitutional monarchy with a representative parliament led by the prime minister's government. It is the only country in the world to have an emperor, whose role is defined by the constitution as symbolising the state and the unity of his people. Japan's parliament, the Diet, is made up of a lower house, the House of Representatives, and an upper house, the House of Councillors. The conservative Liberal Democratic Party, Jiyū-Minshutō (the LDP) is the main party, and it led the country almost without interruption from 1955 to 2009 (except for a short period between 1994 and 1996), and then again in 2012 with the election of Abe Shinzō, successor to the charismatic Koizumi Jun'ichirō (prime minister between 2001 and 2006, known for his passion for Elvis Presley). Between 2009 and 2012 the Democratic Party of Japan, Minshutō (or DPJ), took power. This is a progressive party that in its various forms (it was the old Socialist Party) had long been the second largest party, but in 2017 it split into two. The most important of the other parties is the centre-right Kōmeitō, linked to the secular Buddhist movement Sōka Gakkai which, in its previous incarnation, New Kōmeitō (NKP), formed a coalition government with the LDP. The Japanese Communist Party was founded in 1922 and is the oldest in the Diet. There are various other national and local parties, including the Ainu Party (which has no seats), formed to defend the rights of the minority Ainu people (see 'Of Bears and Men', page 87).

throne in 2019), it is year 2 of the Reiwa era. The system is so confusing that many reporters in Japan carry a handy chart to translate the imperial calendar dates into international time.

Sugano also credits Nippon Kaigi with politically resurrecting Prime Minister Abe, whose career was considered dead after his abrupt resignation in 2007. He also believes their goal may be to radically alter the sections of the constitution which define marriage and the rights of wives, thus 'rolling back sexual equality and making Japan a country pleasant for cranky old men like themselves'.

While several recently published books and articles paint a picture of a masterful Machiavellian organisation that has skirted the law to avoid having to register as a political group, Sugano believes they are primarily reactionary and with no clear idea of what they want to do once their goals are achieved. 'They have worked steadily and stealthily with local politicians and political lobbies to oppose things like gender equality, recognition of war crimes and the comfort women [sex slaves during the Second World War], women using their maiden names after marriage, etc. It's anti-this and anti-that but has no vision of the future.'

Other researchers have taken notice of the group's anti-gender-equality stance but point out that Prime Minister Abe appears to be sincere about promoting women in the workplace and that the group also has female lawmakers in its ranks. Sugano isn't surprised. 'Prime Minister Abe talks a lot about womenomics [the empowerment of women in the business world], but it's all talk. It's like a Texas racist saying, "I have a black friend so I'm not racist." The fact that there are female politicians supported by the group follows the same logic. There are always some minorities in a minority that

Above and below: Every year far-right nationalist groups – including Nippon Kaigi – private citizens and government officials visit the Yasukuni Shrine. Many wear uniforms or clothing linked to the Imperial Army and display the Japanese imperial flag.
Pages 54–5: A man sitting in a kiosk inside the shrine exhibits nationalist paraphernalia.

consider discrimination to be acceptable. Or these women find the support of the group advantageous to themselves – if not for women in general.'

Professor Jeff Kingston, a historian of modern Japan, has pointed out that, while Abe says all the right things, he has quietly reduced from 30 per cent to 15 per cent his original professed goal of promoting women in management, and in reality his meagre actions are 'a nod to patriarchal realities that exposes Abe's version of womenomics as a sham'.

Sugano insists the 'patriarchal realities' of Japan are one reason behind Japanese media's self-censorship under the Abe administration and why they long avoided touching upon Nippon Kaigi. He argues that mainstream Japanese media are run by misogynistic old men whose worldviews align with Nippon Kaigi's sexist ideals, and since they agree with their principles they have seen no need to report on the organisation. 'It is not self-censorship. It's more like silent collusion,' he said.

Nippon Kaigi's dismissive attitude towards women and children also explains its evident opposition to the United Nations Convention on the Rights of the Child (UNCRC). If you ask Sugano why we should be concerned about the influence of Nippon Kaigi, he will tell you why in his Kansai-accented Texas drawl. 'The LDP, Abe and Nippon Kaigi have essentially the same agenda. The frightening thing about this election is that they have never been closer to achieving their dreams – amending the constitution to return Japan to a militaristic feudal society where women, children, youngsters and foreigners, including the Japanese-Koreans, have no basic human rights. They will only have one right: the right to shut up.'

On 10 July 2016 Mari Yamamoto and I published 'The Religious Cult Secretly

ABE SHINZŌ

Abe is descended from a long line of politicians, and, thanks to winning a fourth mandate in the October 2017 elections, he is the longest serving prime minister in Japanese history. His first period of government was short, 2006–7, and was engulfed by scandals linked to two of his agriculture ministers who were forced to resign within a few days of each other. Abe himself then had to resign through problems with ulcerative colitis. His bid for re-election in 2012 was based on the slogan 'Abenomics', an ambitious programme designed to combat Japan's decade of economic stagnation with a hyper-aggressive monetary policy, a series of fiscal stimuli and structural reforms. These measures were effective but still not enough to achieve, for example, the aim of 2 per cent inflation. His third period in office, from 2014 to 2017, was once again dogged by controversy, especially around laws extending the field of intervention of the Japan Self-Defense Forces abroad and those reducing liberties in the name of anti-terrorism. There were also further scandals: in one case a finance minister apparently sold public land very cheaply to a company that ran a conservative private school with whom Abe's wife had connections. In a second case, correspondence emerged that showed the prime minster putting pressure on people in order to get a licence for a company run by a friend of his. A political conservative and a nationalist, Abe has often been criticised for his reactionary positions and his revisionism.

> 'After all is said and done, it must be hard to worship someone – in this case the emperor – who probably despises you.'

Running Japan' in the *Daily Beast*, and it went viral. The upshot was that Nippon Kaigi felt compelled to hold a press conference at the Foreign Correspondent's Club of Japan (FCCJ). The press conference, with Takubo Tadae appearing on behalf of the group, was enlightening.

Takubo, a Kyōrin University professor emeritus specialising in international politics, assumed the Nippon Kaigi chair in 2015. He came to the FCCJ ostensibly to explain why revising the constitution is necessary for modern Japan and to make the case that the group and Prime Minister Abe are not extremists but centralists. Mr Takubo's views are not unknown. In the July 2015 edition of Nippon Kaigi's monthly magazine *Nippon no ibuki*, Takubo noted that 'Abe is a leader that the heavens have bestowed upon us.' He argued that Japan's constitution must be revised while Abe is in office, advocated that Article 9 of the constitution be amended and that the emperor be reinstated as head of state. He also argued for an emergency powers act, which would give the prime minister supreme power in a crisis – something that many critics believe would pave the way for a dictatorship. The implementation of such an act is something the Liberal Democratic Party has been advocating strongly and eerily echoes cabinet minister Asō Tarō's remarks about learning from the Nazis and changing the constitution quietly before anyone notices.

During the press conference Takubo said Japan wasn't entirely wrong to wage the Second World War and some of what they did was right. He did not go into any details of how the war was justified, however. During his reign (1989–2019) Emperor Akihito made several comments which lamented war atrocities committed by the Japanese Army and statements that war must never be waged again. This doesn't quite gel with Nippon Kaigi's desire to whitewash the past and their zeal for making Japan a military power capable of once again conducting a war. It begs the question as to how far Takubo and Nippon Kaigi would be willing to follow the wishes of the emperor. So I asked Takubo if he didn't see a contradiction in worshipping the emperor and ignoring the emperor's comments, but he didn't answer the question at first. Instead he gave a long mini-lecture on Japanese imperial history and the traditional role of the emperor as a Shinto priest-ruler. When asked a second time, 'Do you agree with the emperor's statements on pacifism and [Japan] inflicting harm on the people that Japan conquered, yes or no?' Takubo responded without hesitation, 'Everything the emperor says is correct.'

As previously mentioned, Nippon Kaigi has also repeatedly expressed opposition to the UNCRC, and a senior member of the group, Kase Hideaki, helped found the Association of Corporal Punishment, which advocates physical punishment as a means of educating youth and making them strong. When Takubo was asked why Nippon Kaigi opposes the charter and whether they were pro-corporal punishment, Takubo first had to have clarified what his group's position was. Takubo declined to say that Kase and Nippon

Kaigi's views on child-rearing policy were the same, but that didn't stop him from expressing similar feelings on the issue.

Takubo then paraphrased some reports by Lafcadio Hearn (1850–1904), a writer popular in Japan, who wrote his observations on society during the Russo-Japanese War of 1904–5. 'Hearn observed that Japanese children are allowed to be so free and raucous that even if they cause a commotion in a restaurant they're completely left alone, so there's no corporal punishment in Japan. Hearn also noticed that Japanese society is much tougher on children when they enter university, but corporal punishment should be instilled much earlier to make them behave.' Takubo was hopeful that Japan would adopt a tough-love policy in the future. 'When it comes to children, there should be some corporal punishment, such as spanking if they are misbehaving, just like they do in the United States,' Takubo said.

After the press conference was over Sugano Tamotsu had a few observations. He believed that Takubo's statement put the group in a terrible double bind. 'The emperor and the crown prince [now the Emperor Naruhito] appear to be very much pacifists. If "everything the emperor says is correct" then the group needs to re-evaluate many of its mistaken views. Imagine what happens if the emperor says the pacifist constitution shouldn't be touched.'

Nippon Kaigi is fanatical about reinstalling the emperor as head of state and the need for members of parliament to visit the Yasukuni Shrine to the war dead. Ironically, Emperor Hirohito (1901–89), posthumously known as Emperor Shōwa, seemed to have a strong disdain for nationalist extremists. After it was reported in the 1970s that the Yasukuni Shrine secretly enshrined several class-A Second World War criminals, Emperor Hirohito stopped visiting it.

He never explained why in public. His son, the former Emperor Akihito, has also never visited. Prime Minister Abe visited the shrine in 2013, and his cabinet appointees make a semi-regular practice of doing so.

If the goal of the press conference was to correct the group's image as a religious ultra-nationalist organisation, it couldn't be counted a success. However, they did score emotional points. One couldn't help but feel a twinge of sympathy for the frail-looking Mr Takubo and even some of the other members of Nippon Kaigi. After all is said and done, it must be hard to worship someone – in this case the emperor – who probably despises you. Although Takubo did speak publicly in May 2018 of his support for Abe's proposed constitutional reforms, the group has, for the most part, avoided the limelight since the press conference and appears to be quietly biding its time until Prime Minister Abe can achieve what they've been hoping for. However, the independent documentary *Shusenjo: The Main Battleground of the Comfort Women Issue* (Miki Dezaki, 2019) has recently put the group and its leaders in the spotlight once again, much to their chagrin, and the film is now being shown worldwide. Yet the general public still seems rather unconcerned.

The only substantial obstacle in their path appears, ironically, to be the former emperor, who retired in 2019, and the current emperor, the two individuals that the group wishes to deify but who have no interest and no desire to see a return to Imperial Japan – but neither Nippon Kaigi nor the Japanese prime minister really seem to be paying much attention to the gods.

Mari Yamamoto and Louis Krauss contributed to this article.

Why Is Japan Populist-Free?

The optimistic analysis of a leading expert on Japan is that, despite Prime Minister Abe Shinzō's nationalism, it remains a country rooted in the middle class in which social harmony still prevails. As a result, it has avoided the drift into populism that is now rocking many Western and other nations.

IAN BURUMA

The audience at a performance in a Hawaiian-themed park in Iwaki, Fukushima Prefecture.

Even as a wave of right-wing populism is sweeping Europe, the United States, India, Brazil and parts of Southeast Asia, Japan has so far appeared to be immune. There are no Japanese demagogues like Geert Wilders, Marine Le Pen, Donald Trump, Narendra Modi, Jair Bolsonaro or Rodrigo Duterte, who have exploited pent-up resentments against cultural or political elites. Why?

Perhaps the closest Japan has come was the former mayor of Osaka, Hashimoto Tōru, who first made his name as a television personality and then disgraced himself in recent years by commending the use of wartime sex slaves by the Imperial Japanese Army. His ultra-nationalist views and loathing of liberal media were a familiar version of right-wing populism. But he never managed to break into national politics.

Hashimoto now gives Prime Minister Abe Shinzō free advice on tightening national-security laws. And therein lies one explanation for the apparent lack of right-wing populism in Japan. No one could be more identified with the political elite than Abe, the grandson of a wartime cabinet minister and later prime minister and son of a foreign minister. And yet he shares right-wing populists' hostility to liberal academics, journalists and intellectuals.

Post-war Japanese democracy was influenced in the 1950 and 1960s by a leftist intellectual elite that consciously sought to distance Japan from its wartime nationalism. Abe and his allies are trying to quash that influence. His efforts to revise Japan's pacifist constitution, restore pride in its wartime record and discredit 'elitist' mainstream media, such as the left-of-centre newspaper *Asahi Shimbun*, have earned him the praise of Donald Trump's former strategist Stephen Bannon, who called Abe a Trump before Trump. In some ways Bannon was right to think so. In November 2016 Abe told Trump, 'I've been successful in taming the *Asahi Shimbun*. I hope you will likewise be successful in taming *The New York Times*.' Even as a joke between two supposedly democratic leaders, this was disgraceful.

So one might say that elements of right-wing populism are at the heart of the Japanese government, embodied by a scion of one of the country's most elite families. This paradox, however, is not the only explanation for the absence of a Japanese Le Pen, Modi, Bolsonaro or Wilders.

For demagogues to be able to stir up popular resentments against foreigners, cosmopolitans, intellectuals and liberals there must be wide and obvious financial, cultural and educational disparities. This was the case in Japan in the mid-1930s, when military hotheads staged a failed

IAN BURUMA is a naturalised British writer and academic originally from the Netherlands, who studies Eastern cultures with a particular interest in Japan as well as Chinese literature and Japanese cinema. His published works include *Occidentalism: The West in the Eyes of Its Enemies* (Penguin, 2004), *Murder in Amsterdam: The Death of Theo van Gogh and the Limits of Tolerance* (Atlantic, 2006), *Year Zero: A History of 1945* (Penguin, 2013) and *A Tokyo Romance: A Memoir* (Atlantic/Penguin, 2018).

The audience at a kimono fashion show in a hotel in Ginza, Tokyo.

coup aimed at bankers, businessmen and politicians, who were, in their view, corrupting the Japanese polity. The coup was supported by soldiers who had often grown up in poor rural areas. Their sisters sometimes had to be sold to big-city brothels for their families to survive. The Westernised cosmopolitan urban elites were the enemy – and public opinion was largely on the side of the rebels.

Contemporary Japan may have its flaws, but it is now much more egalitarian than the USA, India or many countries in Europe. High taxes make it hard to pass on inherited wealth. And, unlike in the USA, where material prosperity is flaunted – not least by Trump himself – the most affluent Japanese tend to be discreet. Japan has surpassed the USA as a country of the middle class.

Resentment feeds off a sense of humiliation, a loss of pride. In a society where human worth is measured by individual success, symbolised by celebrity and money, it is easy to feel humiliated by a relative lack of it, of being just another face in the crowd. In extreme cases, desperate individuals will assassinate a president or a rock star just to get into the news. Populists find support among those resentful faces in the crowd, people who feel that elites have betrayed them by taking away their sense of pride in their class, their culture or their race.

This has not happened yet in Japan. Culture may have something to do with

Below: Members of a choir at a centre for the elderly in Tokyo. **Pages 62–3:** The swimming pool at a Hawaiian-themed park in Iwaki on a Sunday in August.

SHOKUNIN

Shokunin is an untranslatable term that is vital in understanding the Japanese work ethic. It means something like 'artisan or craftsman devoted to work', and it is applied in every sector, even to the most humble, repetitive and poorly paid jobs that would be far less respected elsewhere. In Japan, though, every worker seems to be proud of their own contribution to society and committed to giving their best. The spirit of *shokunin* explains the perfectionism, the obsessive attention to detail shared by everyone, from cooks to artisans, and the respect for all white-collar jobs. It also allows people working at supermarket checkouts, call-centre operators and cloakroom attendants to feel less alienated, to feel proud of their work and to have a sense of doing something useful for society. When taken to an extreme, this sense of duty and absolute dedication to the cause can lead to exhaustion and even *karōshi*, death through overwork (see page 140).

> 'There are several reasons why Japanese governments have resisted neo-liberalism: corporate interests, bureaucratic privileges and corrupt politics of various kinds. But preserving pride in employment, at the cost of efficiency, is also one of them.'

it. Self-promotion, in the American style, is frowned upon. To be sure, Japan has a celebrity culture, driven by mass media, but self-worth is defined less by individual fame or wealth than by having a place in a collective enterprise and doing the job to which one is assigned as well as one can.

People in department stores appear to take genuine pride in wrapping merchandise beautifully. Some jobs – think of those uniformed middle-aged men who smile and bow to customers entering a bank – appear to be entirely superfluous. It would be naive to assume that these tasks give huge satisfaction, but they offer people a sense of place, a role in society, however humble.

Meanwhile, the domestic Japanese economy remains one of the most protected and least globalised in the developed world. There are several reasons why Japanese governments have resisted the neo-liberalism promoted in the West since the Reagan/Thatcher years: corporate interests, bureaucratic privileges and corrupt politics of various kinds. But preserving pride in employment, at the cost of efficiency, is also one of them. If this stifles individual enterprise, then so be it.

Thatcherism has probably made the British economy more efficient, but, by crushing trade unions and other established institutions of working-class culture, governments have also taken away sources of pride for people who often do unpleasant jobs. Efficiency does not create a sense of community. Those who now feel adrift blame their predicament on elites who are better educated and sometimes more talented and thus better able to thrive in a global economy. One of the more ironic consequences is that many such people in the USA have chosen as their president a narcissistic billionaire who brags about his wealth, personal success and genius. Nothing like that is likely to happen in Japan. We might learn something valuable from reflecting on the reasons why.

Why Is Japan Populist-Free?

Yoshimoto Banana
A Simple Thank You

Translated by Meredith McKinney

Yoshimoto Banana's love letter to Shimokitazawa, the area of Tokyo where she has lived for many years, provides her with the opportunity to reflect on the emotions and memories bound up in her house but also on the indifference underpinning contemporary Japan's systems of insurance and service provision.

A view over the Shimokitazawa district of Tokyo.

YOSHIMOTO BANANA, the daughter of Yoshimoto Takaaki, one of Japan's most famous intellectuals, has, in her turn, become one of her country's leading writers, garnering a huge readership since her debut with *Kitchen* (first published in Japanese in 1988 and in English in 1993), a literary sensation that has sold more than 5 million copies worldwide. Other novels published in English include *Amrita* (Grove Press, 1997), *Asleep* (Grove Press, 2000), *Goodbye Tsugumi* (Grove Press, 2002) and *Moshi Moshi* (Counterpoint, 2016).

I've had reason to move house again, this time to a place one station on from Shimokitazawa. So my nearest city – if you could call it a city – is still Shimokitazawa.

This feels like the last move I'll ever undertake, and it was particularly emotional in all kinds of ways. The haunting sense that this just might be the place where I die; the gut-wrenching thought that the animals who live with me will no doubt die here, too.

It's the first time I've had such feelings about where I live, and for this very reason I have a presentiment that these things will indeed come to pass. This house will be the base from which I'll set off and to which I'll return.

The first time I entered this house I had the conviction that this was the place I'd seen in my dreams for such a long time. That conviction stayed with me throughout the move. All flowed smoothly, and questions of money, of time and all the other various difficulties somehow turned out just fine. The child-me who lives within sat for a while hugging her knees miserably, unable at first to adjust to the change. But my animals, who'd protested at the last move, quickly settled in this time, and things flowed along nicely and according to schedule. The move was tough, yes, but this time around I wasn't struggling against the flow, so the damage was minimal.

Itchan and Masako, who came to help, carried in and set up my precious objects with wonderful sympathy and care. The carpenter and the gardener, old friends of mine, did sterling work. Even though it was midwinter they didn't stint on labour; they saw to the construction of the house and placing of the plants in the garden with the same infinite care they would have given to their own homes. Even now when I think of this I'm close to tears.

I also had a great many unusual experiences this time in my real estate and bank dealings, often very happy and fortuitous ones. The site manager's note saying 'Thank you for making me coffee; it was delicious' made me smile; the architect's tales of his early childhood filled me with a desire to care for this house of his. The estate agent was not only smart but an interesting man, and the whole family became great fans.

*

The business of real estate had changed in a number of ways in the years since my last experience of that world.

The fact is that, no matter how careful you are, either when renting or buying, the individual is always on the losing side of the deal. There's nothing you can do about it. Individuals are simply in a weak position. In these times, when business transactions always involve a certain amount of rip-off, putting the breach-of-promise clause in tiny print is one of the less unethical behaviours.

To give you an example, the contract for the house I sold had a clause stating 'ten-year guarantee against flaws in construction' with an additional clause to cover any interim change of title holder called a 'special resale agreement'. This guarantee against flaws means that in the case of leaks or deterioration of materials, which are clearly the responsibility of the builder, the insurer is required via the estate agent to foot the bill for repairs. But, as it turns out, if the builder or the estate agent chooses to dig their heels in and to resist, the result is that you can't register a different

---

AN ODE TO SHIMOKITAZAWA

Shimokitazawa is an area of Tokyo's Setagaya district, about three kilometres west of Shibuya, home to (probably) the world's busiest pedestrian crossing, the Shibuya Crossing. Described by many as Tokyo's hippest neighbourhood, in recent years Shimokitazawa has become very popular among young people thanks to its numerous vintage and twentieth-century design shops, old-fashioned stores, family-run restaurants, bars, nightspots and underground theatres. In the mostly traffic-free streets you can enjoy a peaceful, intimate atmosphere sometimes reminiscent of a bygone Japan. Yoshimoto Banana has lived in the area for many years and chose it as the setting for one of her best-known novels, 2010's *Moshi Moshi* (Counterpoint, 2016). In 2016 she published *Shimokitazawa ni tsuite*, a collection of nineteen texts devoted to her neighbourhood and from which this article is taken: memories, encounters, anecdotes and thoughts that convey the unexpected happiness she discovered there.

title holder so that 'special resale agreement' is in fact not legally enforceable.

None of this did I hear about when I signed. When I bought the place it was, 'Don't worry, there's a resale agreement so you can sell any time and the guarantee remains. Looking forward to future dealings with you …' and off they went with the money. Then, later, it was, 'Oh no that won't be possible. The construction company doesn't accept a change of registered owner's name these days, you see … blah, blah, blah,' and I realised I'd been had.

By chance I've moved somewhere not far away so the problem isn't so acute, but if I'd gone to some other part of the country or overseas, as legal title holder I'd have to come flying back whenever something went wrong, employ the contractors to do the work, oversee repairs and so forth.

So just what is this 'ten-year guarantee'? I'd like to know.

You're the one who signed the contract, so you're the one who does it all now. It's nothing to do with us. But when it comes to inspections and the rest, where we stand to gain, we'll be in there like a flash … And these swindlers are probably still there brazenly selling property today. Of course, it's not just this estate agent. I've heard that all the major building firms do similar things. In other words, this kind of semi-legal rip-off is now absolutely standard.

Gone are the days when you built a solid, habitable house, sold it to someone who was happy to buy it and if that person sold it on you would continue to feel responsible for what you'd built and maintain an ongoing arrangement to look after it. Now it's more like, 'Thank heavens. So far they're being acquiescent and nodding obligingly.' People my age can only shake their heads in wonder. This is not just a case of Good Old Days nostalgia – after all, many things today are better than they used to be.

But I have a feeling it's a big mistake to assume that today's system will continue as it is for ever. As long as people are people, those who are out to pull the wool over our eyes will come to grief sooner or later, just as nuclear power in Japan came to grief.

I've written about this elsewhere, but the fact is that, unless humans treat other humans as human, something sometime will have to give.

Take the much-loathed sub-contractors who make what money they can through a process whereby a property-maintenance check is pretty much the equivalent of a fault-finding exercise. And the companies that shamelessly suck that money out of them without getting their own hands dirty.

Or the on-site subcontractors who put together the furniture or install the air conditioners in these places, working to a strict schedule that dictates how much has to be done each day. If they make a mistake it's taken out of their pay, so their only option is to knock themselves out working as fast as they can while making damn sure they never slip up then move on to the next job.

This is an age where a bank will recommend to someone of eighty-five that he put his money in a ten-year-term deposit that only pays interest at full term.

In this land of ours, someone from a bank or insurance company will go knocking on the doors of elderly people living alone to try to lift their money by getting them to sign up for things. All smiles and kindness, they get the insurance money out of you, then when you go into hospital it turns out there's some exclusion clause in the contract that means you get nothing.

Japan is different from America where there's all that land to go around. We just can't do things the same way here. But I have a feeling that, although the way you get swindled in other countries may be more merciless, at least the approach to it is more straightforward than in Japan.

One good thing about the Japanese is that here you'll occasionally come across someone who can actually transcend all this right there on-site, the kind of person who's capable of changing the world from the ground up. That's why you can allow yourself to have hope.

'Everyone's doing it, and we all have to put food on the table, so

A street in Shimokitazawa.

there's no point in thinking about it too deeply,' you may say. But that is a big mistake. Why? Because always and everywhere, then as now, what we're dealing with is still other human beings.

Humans want to be happy, they want peace of mind, they want to maintain friendly relations with honest people. So long as this continues to be the case, whenever and wherever you are, you'll find the great principle of cause-and-effect at work – that universal, unalterable karmic law of retribution that says you reap as you sow.

*

Whenever I see a staircase I think of my mother.

When she could no longer walk, we installed a stair-lift in the family home.

My mother would have her meals in the downstairs guest room, then, when she got tired of sitting there, she'd climb on to the lift and ascend to her bedroom on the second floor. Up she'd sail with a smile and a wave and the words, 'Well, see you later', accompanied by the jingle that played to announce that the lift was in motion.

Her beaming face was reminiscent of some young starlet leaving the stage.

It is a great sorrow to me that my poor highly strung mother lived a life that held very few such smiles, and it feels to me like a blessing from above that once a bit of dementia had crept up on her she spent her days smiling. A certain degree of relaxation does seem to be more conducive to human happiness.

Well, anyway, no sooner had I moved into the new house than I fell down the stairs.

I was somewhat exhausted from the days of hard work. I wasn't paying attention, and I was flustered because I had to get ready to go to the airport.

Down I went with incredible momentum, striking my coccyx hard on the stairs as I fell. When I checked in the mirror, I was astonished to see that my backside now looked as if it was neatly divided into four thanks to the horizontal bruise across it.

I wept from the pain. The dog delighted me by coming over to lick me. But I couldn't stand and I couldn't sit, and whatever I did my head just screamed 'Ow!'

Nevertheless, once I could walk a little I set off as planned to Hokkaido. I yelped with pain as the plane touched down, and once I reached the hotel I developed a fever and took to my bed. Outside was a frozen world of wildly swirling snow. My spirits plummeted, but nevertheless I dragged myself along as promised to the Sapporo headquarters of the Magic Spice Restaurant.

This is a soup curry restaurant that also has a branch in Shimokitazawa near where I live. The owner, Shimomura-san, is an intrepid fellow who has been abducted in Thailand, been a practising psychic and has generally followed a chequered career path to finally arrive at what his fate dictated – bringing health to others through spicy curries. The chaotic glitter inside his restaurant holds all the glorious complexity of that world of his.

You could read a book about him and never really grasp intellectually what he's about, but you only have to meet him to know what a sharp yet serene and thoroughly warm-hearted person he is. His daughter is a well-known singer who goes by the name of Hitomitoi. I just love her delicate voice. His wife is too cute for words and shines like the sun. The whole family gets on famously together, radiating a sense of natural harmony.

Perhaps it was the power of Shimomura-san's karma, perhaps it was the kindly welcome, but, although I'd barely managed to stagger there in considerable pain, just sitting eating a bowl of soup curry I felt my spirits rise and my health returning till I felt so much better that, for all the agony, I was happy.

When I mentioned how it hurt, Shimomura-san and his wife produced a precious ointment they'd bought in Thailand, and when it was time to leave they helped me carefully back down the stairs. It stirred in me the vivid memory of the touch of my gentle mother and father. That may have been what really did the trick.

The first time I was somewhat surprised by the astonishing number of vegetables in Magic Spice curries, their special Hokkaido sweetness, the attitude of the waiters. I found myself wondering if I could maybe play the tourist and just give the food a try.

But, as I continued to call in there, I'd find myself thinking happily on the walk back, I actually like to eat lots of vegetables. And think of all the good spices I've had. I've been warmly greeted and well treated. I liked the place more and more. That extra sweetness now seemed to hold a deep tenderness. It's always a happy thing to witness the realisation of a world born out of someone's imagination, and that was what it felt like inside that restaurant. I felt it was a place with deep roots – not the kind of place created from some received idea or according to some vague concept of 'Asian style' but a place where everything was there for a reason and had come from somewhere deep. That's how it felt to me.

My coccyx still hurt, but I felt just fine in myself.

This was because there was real love in that food. The friends I went with, who looked after me with such real concern; the quiet encouragement of Shimomura-san and his wife; the brisk efficiency of the waiters – all these things penetrated my heart in the same way love does. Outside the windows was a world of the whitest snow where, for someone such as myself, unused to such conditions, it was all too easy to slip and compound my problems by hitting my poor sore coccyx again. Yet, somehow, I felt safe.

You receive love, you return thanks – what goes around comes around.

This is the essence of human relations, lightening the load of even the weightiest problems that burden each individual. How good it would be if only this was the way the world was.

*

The house I lived in for just a little while – the one with that fine guarantee that didn't work – was a very good place to be.

I had been through a truly gruelling experience when I moved in there; there I talked with my family, there I made myself sleepless with thinking, there I became a serious person and it was from there that I set out on all those occasions to visit Funabashi, the setting for the novel I wanted to write.

The house was so small that I couldn't bring myself to contemplate spending the rest of my life there with the family, but, transients though we were, it held us tenderly within its walls. No problems ever arose there, and a bright, gentle, sweet air always flowed through it.

I remember the hot rainless summer evening one year when I came staggering back, dog-tired, from Funabashi and walked home from Setagaya Daita station. I greeted dear old Mrs Yamazaki, and my sandalled feet trudged on. My hands held a loaf of bread I'd bought at Funabashi.

Ah, I was thinking, at last I've gathered all the material I need from Funabashi. It's been such fun. It's kind of sad it's over. I'll enjoy finishing the novel, but I won't be getting off at Funabashi any more with that sense that somehow I live there ... and I looked up at my house.

There, beneath the summer sky, it seemed to be beaming a welcome to me. There were the huge lotus leaves and my family's name on the plate. Light flooded the building; the white of the walls glowed.

This was a space that had always loved us, 100 per cent.

The thought of letting it go was so frightening I wanted to weep, but then the new is always frightening.

Once I'm settled into *this* house I'm sure I'll go on to write many more things.

This house isn't like that last gentle one. This is a house of power, a place of sharp edges in all sorts of ways – it was, after all, able to throw me down the stairs. There's a certain severe atmosphere that tells you it means serious business; it can see how infantile we are, and it's not about to relax and soften up just yet. I get the feeling it will take time for us to get to know one another, but that's what makes it such an honest and trustworthy place.

The first night we moved in we plugged in the TV, and we a watching it and eating takeaway pizza together. Looking at the friends and family I love, I was flooded with the thought that this really was our house.

And yet, brief though it was, that wonderful time in the other house remains with me.

That day when I went out on to the veranda just as the old lady next door emerged, and we stood there chatting, gossiping about the neighbourhood, both dressed in little more than our pyjamas.

The old lady who came around collecting funds for the neighbourhood association who was always so tired, but when I offered to help she smiled with that carefully painted bright-red mouth of hers and declared that if she didn't have this work to do she was convinced she'd turn senile.

The charming family that was always taking walks with their dog and cat in tow.

It hurts to think that this minor relocation of mine has wrenched me from that life where I lived in the same rhythm as those people.

*

But I want to live this moment, this day, looking up, looking forward.

It reminds me of how I can yearn for the time when my son was still a baby, and catching sight of the toys and the picture books I read him every day as a child can smite my heart, but there's more delight in meeting him as he is now.

The fact is, the time I have in this life is only now.

Goodbye my dear, tiny, sweet old home. I just want to say thank you. 🖋

Murakami Ryū
The Withering of Desire

Translated by Meredith McKinney

The inability to be moved, the decline in desire and the growth in cases of depression are examined by a leading light of Japanese literature, Murakami Ryū, who wonders whether the socio-economic instability that hit in the late 1980s could be responsible for many transformations in Japanese society.

The public housing complex (*danchi*) in Takashimadaira known as the 'suicide *danchi*' because of the number of people who have attempted suicide by jumping from the upper storeys of its buildings; protective nets have now been installed to prevent this.

MURAKAMI RYŪ is a Japanese writer, essayist and screenwriter. He grew up in contact with Western culture through a US military base and made his debut in 1976 with *Almost Transparent Blue* (1976; first translated into English in 1977), winning a number of major awards. He has also directed five films based on his novels. Other works translated into English include *In the Miso Soup* (Kodansha, 2004) and *Tokyo Decadence* (Kurodahan, 2016).

79

Some years ago I gave the title *Jisatsu yori wa SEX* – which translates as 'Sex Rather than Suicide' – to a collection of essays on the theme of women and love (published by KK Bestsellers, 2003; not published in English). Believing as I do that suicide is a terrible thing, I considered using the title 'Murder Rather Than Suicide', but I chose sex in the end because the alternative was simply too dangerous. This was when the theme of the essays underwent a subtle shift.

Take the Japanese phenomenon of *gōkon*, for instance, which is where a group of young singles get together to pair off. I used to be quite unsympathetic and critical of young women who indulged in this. I said outright that they shouldn't do it, that it was wrong.

I must admit I've never had first-hand experience of *gōkon*. For one thing I'm well known, so I have to be careful how I behave in public. More to the point, though, faced with a bunch of women I would be meeting for the first time I wouldn't know what to talk about. For a long time I felt that it was incredibly sad to look for a lover or marriage partner through *gōkon* – and that, fundamentally, remains my opinion – but I now think that if, instead of slipping into a suicidal state of mind, you can make yourself happy by finding a lover through *gōkon*, well, so be it.

The same goes for cosmetic surgery. I used to think that you shouldn't mess around with your face and body with surgery but instead persevere and bolster your confidence – and that, fundamentally, remains my opinion. But if your appearance causes such problems with interpersonal relations that you lose all confidence, find yourself in an unhappy mental state and start considering suicide, I now think it's unquestionably better to undergo cosmetic surgery.

And what about those who work in the adult-entertainment industries? Are they to blame? The now-obsolete *enjo kōsai* (sugar-daddy dating, all the rage a few decades ago) or housewife prostitutes might be considered morally wrong, but more important are the attendant risks of illness or getting caught up in crime, and, above all, there's the evil of selling oneself cheap. This was the theme of my novel *Rabu ando poppu* ('Love and Pop'; Gentōsha, 1996; not published in English). But they're better than suicide.

I also used to be critical of Japan's brand-name worship. I wrote essays about how young women in the main western-European countries don't own Louis Vuitton handbags and the rest, and I said the same sort of thing in interviews. I wrote about how, particularly in Italy and France, many non-famous makers produce handbags of superior design and function so young women have no need of exclusive branded bags such as those of Louis Vuitton. My opinion remains the same today. But if having a Louis Vuitton handbag will improve the way you feel, well, so be it.

*

It's not that I'm any less radical in my way of thinking or that age has smoothed off the edges, it's just that I've realised there's something else that must take priority. Recent years have seen a marked increase in clinical depression in Japan. Per head of population

---

GETTING TOGETHER IN TIMES OF CRISIS

In Japan, a *gōkon* is a group blind date for people hoping to meet a partner or even just to make friends. Generally, a man and a woman who know each other organise the *gōkon* in advance, each of them agreeing to bring three or four suitable friends with them, with the aim of forming a group with the same number of men and women. They usually meet in an *izakaya*, a restaurant where people can eat, drink, chat and flirt. The term *gōkon* dates back to the 1970s and derives from the Japanese words *konpa* (from the German word *Kompanie* – company in English – meaning a party for members of a group, class or club) and *gōdō*, 'together'. In a country where 35 per cent of men in their thirties have never had a girlfriend and the number of single people is constantly rising, *gōkon* are intended to give people the opportunity to make friends and possibly form long-term relationships. This type of event is an established fixture in Japanese society, beginning at university and continuing into the world of work, where extremely busy schedules and a demanding, competitive corporate culture mean time for meeting people is decidedly limited.

the numbers are still low compared with the rest of the world, but there's no denying the sudden dramatic increase, and the rates continue to rise. Japan's suicide rate per one hundred thousand is the highest in the developed world. There's no question that it's better to buy Louis Vuitton handbags, to have cosmetic surgery, to go to *gōkon* parties or sell your body if the alternative is depression that leads to suicide. Today, with the Japanese economy still in the doldrums, salaries kept low and our society rife with forebodings that the future holds no improvement, the most important thing is to ensure that we remain healthy and to prevent mental states that provoke thoughts of suicide.

Apparently it's important for the prevention of depression to be able to tell yourself that, although the bad times seem likely to continue, somehow things will work out. Mustering your courage to believe this and looking on the bright side – optimism of this sort is vital, a psychologist friend informs me. But it's not that easy to do. In order to believe things will work out you need the experience of things having worked out before. When you think about it, everyone alive today has survived this far without dying, so in a sense things have worked out for all of us, but one could argue that simply not dying isn't really enough.

*

There's a branch of the supermarket chain Seijō Ishii near my house where I often go to shop. The place is stacked with alcoholic drinks, from Western wines to Japanese sake, and an abundance of imported foodstuffs lines the shelves. As I was queuing at the cash register the other day my gaze fell on an old man cradling a bottle of excellent Koshi no Kagetora sake as tenderly as one would a child. To judge from his clothes and shoes he was far from wealthy. Our eyes met, so I nodded towards the bottle and remarked that he had a fine drink there. The old man's face lit up, and he gave a mischievous chuckle. Noting the packet of dried cuttlefish clutched in his right hand, I guessed that he was happily anticipating snacking on it while he drank his Kagetora sake later that night. It put me in a good mood, too.

The old fellow looked to be well into his eighties, and if he could still enjoy a bottle of sake at that age he must be in reasonable health. He wouldn't be able to indulge himself like that if he had any worries about his blood-sugar levels, for instance. Needless to say, he must be someone who loved his sake and was aware of that fact – the fact that he liked a drink, I mean. Perhaps he'd carefully squirrelled away money from his pension to buy his bottle of Kagetora or taken on some part-time work so he could afford it.

I'd say it was his special treat to himself to settle down with a bottle of Kagetora and a snack. The reason this put me in such good spirits is that it's a rare sight nowadays. You almost never see someone who simply accepts their own desire and eagerly looks forward to satisfying it. Think of the clientele in hotel bars. How many such people do you see there?

Maybe people just aren't getting so excited about things these days. Maybe we're losing the prerequisite for that kind of

PLATONIC LOVE

According to a 2017 survey of Japanese people aged between eighteen and thirty-five, 42 per cent of unmarried men and 44 per cent of unmarried women had never had sex (over 50 per cent of men and over 60 per cent of women get married between the ages of thirty and thirty-four). Not only that, 70 per cent of unmarried men and 60 per cent of unmarried women were not in a relationship, and only a third of married couples had sexual relations once a week. So why are people not having more sex? Work exhaustion, certainly, a wish to avoid the emotional complications of being in a relationship, but it is also down to demographics and the economic crisis.

Bear in mind that around 28 per cent of the population is over sixty-five, which is the highest proportion in the world. It is difficult to find reliable data, but it seems that the Japanese sex industry, which is more culturally accepted than elsewhere, is trying to appeal to older people by adapting to satisfy the desires of citizens who are increasingly uninterested in carnal pleasures. As a result, 'softer' services are gaining popularity to the detriment of more explicit offerings. According to Pornhub, the largest adult-video website, the Japanese are fourth in the world in terms of traffic, but the ranking of most searched-for terms is revealing: after 'lesbian' comes 'hentai', which refers to anime (cartoons) rather than pornographic videos featuring real people.

excitement where the heart races in anticipation, like it used to do when you were a child the night before an excursion. To look forward excitedly to something, you need desire. And it seems to me that desire itself is disappearing from contemporary Japanese society. It has been many years now since I met a young person who spoke of any urgent desire to *do* something. Mind you, desires and aspirations tend to diminish if you proclaim them too easily to others. It's not as though that old guy in the supermarket came right out and announced, 'Actually, the thing I love most of all is drinking sake and snacking on dried cuttlefish.' No, you catch hints of someone's desires or aspirations in their behaviour and appearance. You don't really hear it expressed in regular conversation, let alone loudly proclaimed to untold numbers of people using a megaphone in front of the railway station. You don't feel any personal desire behind the words of the politician who stands there shouting to passers-by, 'I will do my absolute best for the sake of your happiness!' What he is actually saying is that he wants your vote and he takes no real responsibility.

Why is desire withering? Is it because the Japanese economy is stagnant? Is it because society has matured to the point where scarcity and hunger are no longer with us? Yet I don't feel any desire in the homeless who lack so much. Nor can I imagine a homeless man or woman ablaze with desire. It's not desire they give off, it's resignation.

Of Bears
and Men

CESARE ALEMANNI
Translated by Katherine Gregor

For centuries the Ainu, an ancient people from the island of Hokkaido, lived alongside but apart from the rest of the Japanese. Labelled a 'prehistoric aberration' and subjected to repression in the twentieth century, they resisted assimilation thanks to the strength of their traditions – so successfully that now, following a historic court case against the central government, they are being rediscovered by historians, anthropologists ... and tourists.

Pages 86–7: Ainu elder Urakawa Haruzo in his *cise*, the traditional Ainu dwelling, which he built himself in the mountains of Chiba, outside Tokyo (left); a totem carved with animal motifs outside the Poroto Kotan Museum in Shiraoi, Hokkaido (right).

One Sunday in March I take a stroll down a long, wide avenue in the Shinagawa district of Tokyo, so long and wide that, by European standards, it could be a motorway. Halfway through my absent-minded walk I notice a large sign three metres up from the ground, one of the few in English translation. The white lettering on the navy-blue background informs you that in the case of a powerful earthquake the lane nearest the pavement on which I am walking is reserved for rescue vehicles. Besides making me shudder slightly with the reminder that I am treading on one of the most seismic lands in the world, what strikes me is the picture beneath the message. A large catfish, drawn in manga style: white body, red eyes, yellow whiskers. Despite its pictorial stillness, it gives the impression that it is wriggling, as though it has just been hurled out of the water by an invisible hand. And it's smiling a friendly, chubby-cheeked smile. A reminder of how, here in Japan, even life's most terrible events must be dressed in thick layers of *kawaii*, a childish 'cuteness'. I wonder about the connection between the two things – the fish and the message about the earthquake – until, right there and then, I remember a local myth according to which the entire Japanese archipelago rests on the back of a huge catfish. And it is this very catfish that allegedly causes earthquakes by shaking every now and then. Further research suggests that the myth is quite a recent one, dating to the very late Edo period (1603–1868) – 1855 to be precise – after the three great 'Ansei earthquakes' had struck Japan, causing tens of thousands of casualties. The fish has a name, Namazu; before Namazu the role had been 'played' for centuries by a far more menacing dragon, a symbol imported from China. Namazu's cute face on the sign is therefore proof of its uncommon historical resilience in a setting, like that of contemporary Japan, in which the relationship between mythology, tradition and the past is a highly complex one.

This is something known to the very ancient Ainu people, who have been living for thousands of years mainly in Hokkaido, the northernmost island of the Japanese archipelago in the southern part of the Sea of Okhotsk, just a strip of ocean away from the Russian coast. Ethnically distinct from the Yamato people – the stock from which most Japanese come – the Ainu developed a society that is independent from that of their neighbours on Honshu, the main island in the archipelago. Back in 1200, at the time of first contact with the Yamato Japanese – who had started to colonise the south of Hokkaido to flee from a famine afflicting

CESARE ALEMANNI is a writer, journalist and communication consultant, with a career that has included stints as editor-in-chief of Italian magazines *Rivista Studio*, *Prismo* and *Il Tascabile*. Between 2013 and 2016 he founded and ran the international English-language magazine *The Berlin Quarterly*.

KAIJŪ

In Japanese folklore from the early Edo period (1603–1868) the *kaijin* was a monstrous creature that lived in the waters off the Japanese archipelago. Emerging from the sea at night, half man and half amphibian, it terrorised the inhabitants of coastal villages. Later, in the early decades of the twentieth century, slightly mutated into *kaijū*, the term came back into fashion to describe the bones of dinosaurs and other extinct creatures unearthed by palaeontologists. From there it was extended to cover a genre of films that became very popular in post-war Japan and also attracted a cult following in the West: films such as the endless *Godzilla* series, which began in 1954 and continues to this day, *Rodan* (1956) and *Gamera* (1965), typically featuring an enormous monster, often resembling a dinosaur, that emerges from the depths to devastate entire cities and terrify their inhabitants. Made on a low budget, with highly innovative special effects, *kaijū* films also reflected a sort of cathartic processing of the trauma suffered by Japan in 1945 when atomic bombs were dropped on Hiroshima and Nagasaki. In fact, the explanations for the appearance of the enormous creatures in question were often, directly or indirectly, linked with US atomic testing in the Pacific.

Honshu – the Ainu were primarily fishermen, hunters and foragers, who used systems of barter trade and practised animism.

Chronicles of early exchanges between the Yamato and the Ainu, mostly written by the Yamato, reveal the deep sense of surprise that accompanied these encounters. With features closer to those of ethnic groups in what is now far-eastern Russia than their Honshu neighbours, the Ainu were a puzzle to the Yamato incomers. Who were they? Where did they come from, these individuals with faces, customs and social structures that were different from those developed in the rest of the archipelago? That in their native language *ainu* simply meant 'humans' did nothing to help shed light on this question. On the other hand, the fact that even today the Ainu commonly refer to the Japanese with a word of Chinese origin (*wajin*) that means 'coloniser' in an openly negative sense tells us a lot about how they perceived the newcomers and about the balance of power between the two ethnic groups.

At the beginning of the twentieth century, when the whole of Japan was under strict sanctions imposed under a political ideology marked by nationalism, the resistance of many Ainu communities was a source of embarrassment for the central government in Tokyo. Unable to fully resolve this problem and resorting to forced assimilation – if not open and violent oppression – for many decades Japanese political culture was characterised by a kind of negligence of the Ainu issue. Labelled an 'anthropological mystery', a 'dying race' and a 'prehistoric aberration', the Ainu were increasingly marginalised by Hokkaido society.

It is only since the beginning of the new millennium, and partly thanks to pressure from the international community, that

Tokyo's attitude towards the Ainu has changed for the better. As often happens in Japan, the change of direction has been both unexpected and drastic. And so, just a few years after that historical turning point, Ainu culture is now not only protected and encouraged but the traditions and origins of this people have become one of the most popular and competitive study topics among archaeologists and anthropologists – and not just Japanese ones.

There have been two crucial factors in the 'rediscovery' of Ainu culture. First, the Ainu filed a lawsuit against the Japanese government in the late 1980s following plans to build a dam on land they hold sacred. Although the final verdict, passed by Judge Ichimiya Kazuo in 1997, did not stop work on the dam, it nevertheless marked the first and previously unheard-of step towards recognising the Ainu as a people with culture and traditions that were distinct from the Yamato Japanese. Moreover, the verdict adhered to a more general rethinking of the relationship between contemporary Japan and its past. During the post-war years the country had set off on a wild race for modernisation to the detriment of its own traditions and history, which led it briefly to compete with

Clockwise from left:
High-school student Maya poses with a fishing rod; prayer sticks used in Ainu ceremonies; a view in the Noboribetsu Bear Park, Hokkaido.

the United States to be number one in the world economy (nowadays it ranks third). Apart from being economically motivated, this leap forward was also a way of forgetting the humiliating defeat of the Second World War and the two atom bombs. At the same time there was a desire to erase the memory of the war crimes committed by Japanese imperialism in China, Korea and Taiwan at the beginning of the last century, in particular during the first twenty years of Hirohito's reign (also known as the Shōwa era), which lasted from 1926 to 1989. The ongoing stagnation of the Japanese economy, which began in the 1990s, has slowed the pace of society overall and allowed for a window to be opened to re-examine of the past. This includes a decade-old controversy over the textbooks adopted by high-school teachers, almost all of which still play down the atrocities perpetrated by Japanese soldiers during the country's expansionist years in Indochina and the fact that air force pilots were driven to become kamikaze through coercion and subtle psychological torture. It is therefore understandable that, within this delicate and complex cultural debate, what is after all a secondary issue like the Ainu should have encountered a more favourable and indulgent climate in recent decades than in the past.

The recent scientific interest is also a result of this progress, and some of the mysteries in which these people have long been shrouded are finally clearing to reveal answers. For example, we now know that the ancestors of the Ainu probably came to Hokkaido about twenty thousand years ago across a land bridge thought to have existed during the Würm glaciation (the most recent ice age, 110,000–10,000 BCE). They probably originated in Kamchatka, where a hundred or so Ainu who are acknowledged by the local authorities still live along with another thousand or so that the Russian government does not recognise officially.

Searching for milder southern climes (at least compared with the ones from which they came), the Ainu settled in northern Hokkaido but, once there, encountered harsh temperatures and unyielding soil, too hard and snowy to encourage the development of a farming society, and for a long time they lived by fishing, hunting and gathering wild plants. This primitive way of life did not change until the seventh century CE when, according to recent archaeological discoveries, the Ainu began to develop a more complex sedentary society, partly thanks to contact with other peoples and the creation of a trading network that stretched from northern Korea to Siberia and relied principally on the bartering of goods made from the bones of large animals such as seals, sea lions, whales and bears.

It is impossible to talk about Ainu history without mentioning *Ursus arctos yesoensis*, a brown-bear subspecies native to Hokkaido, slightly smaller in size than the American grizzly but no less fierce a predator. For the Ainu, whose diet historically consists mainly of salmon, the bear was as much a rival as a companion and a protector of fishing – a dual figure that occupied prime position in the Ainu belief system. Its centrality has its roots in the distant past – and this has been confirmed by the recent discovery of *arctos yesoensis* remains, mainly skulls, in a few burial places that date back to 1,000 BCE, at a time when the Ainu performed rituals involving these bears many centuries before first coming into contact with the Yamato.

In the Ainu language, the spirit of the bear is a *kamuy*, a divine essence that belongs to a rich and complex religious pantheon in which every existing entity – animated or not – is in constant balance

URSUS ARCTOS YESOENSIS

A sub-species of *Ursus arctos lasiotus*, commonly known as the brown or grizzly bear, *Ursus arctos yesoensis* is a bear native to Hokkaido, certain forests in North Korea, eastern China and the Russian island of Sakhalin. With a population of around ten thousand on the island of Hokkaido alone, it is the most widespread and populous sub-species of brown bear in the whole of Asia after *Ursus arctos beringianus*, which lives in the far east of Russia and on the Kamchatka Peninsula. Generally smaller, lighter and with a more elongated skull than its western relatives, the bear predominantly eats roots, acorns, wild fruit, small mammals and freshwater fish, particularly salmon. Although the average weight is around two hundred kilograms, in recent years, those studying the animal have observed ever-increasing numbers of much more powerful bears, weighing almost six hundred kilograms. This is a similar weight to the planet's largest grizzly, the Alaskan Kodiak bear (*Ursus arctos middendorffi*), which can weigh as much as eight hundred kilograms. Because of deforestation in Hokkaido, the frequency of encounters between bears and people has grown significantly over the past century, helping to create a climate of hostility and paranoia among local human populations with regard to the animal, which is, nevertheless, considered a protected species.

between two dimensions, physical and spiritual. The physical realm, the world as we know it, is called *ainu mosir* – interestingly, it is also balanced on the back of a huge fish. The spiritual realm, where divine essences live, is called *kamuy mosir*. The two dimensions coexist but in radically separate ways and meet only when a creature dies in the physical world. At this point its spirit is set free from its earthly prison, leaves its resources at the disposal of those who stay behind and travels freely throughout the spiritual world, from where it can exercise positive as well as negative effects on the residents of the physical world.

When a bear dies, not only are its physical remains valuable and highly sought-after (its fur has an unparalleled ability to protect from the cold) but, according to the Ainu, its spiritual aspect is especially important. In order to ensure the bear spirit's benevolence towards them, the Ainu have over the centuries developed a complex ritual called *iyomante*. This involves capturing a bear cub that is then taken care of like a new member of the village. Once it has grown so large and strong that twenty men can no longer handle it, the young bear is sacrificed in a ritual in which it is killed with two arrows then beheaded: a practice that symbolises the fact that the physical prison of its body has been removed and its spirit is free to travel to *kamuy mosir*. Grateful for this liberation, the bear leaves its flesh and its skin to the village that raised it and, alongside this, its eternal benevolence: it becomes a kind of local patron.

Naturally, this cruel ritual is no longer practised and, in general, for all its resistance to modernity, Ainu culture has not completely avoided the taming processes of our times. When you visit Ainu villages, for instance, you will frequently come across soft toy bears designed to appeal to tourists coming to Hokkaido, intrigued by the customs of these bear worshippers. It earns money for the locals but ignores the fact that, for Ainu ancestors, reproducing the animal in a realistic way would have been tantamount to imprisoning its spirit for eternity. It is a small but significant illustration of how cultural assimilation has succeeded by means of economy and tourism where it had failed through politics.

These recent developments notwithstanding, the history of Ainu culture and its relationship with the Yamato establishment – which went from isolation to racism to today's extreme protection – is an eloquent example of how, under the cover of apparent harmony, Japan still has internal differences. Even the Japanese have trouble detecting these from a distance or if they only spend time in large cities. They are differences that the Japanese themselves have for some time tried to erase.

The symbiosis that the Ainu have established with the bear illustrates the history of the relationship between this animal, the island of Hokkaido and its inhabitants – in particular the 'new' Yamato colonisers.

'The physical realm is called *ainu mosir*. The spiritual realm, where divine essences live, is called *kamuy mosir*. The two dimensions coexist but in radically separate ways and meet only when a creature dies in the physical world.'

THE AINU HERO: KAYANO SHIGERU

Kayano Shigeru (1926–2016) is without question one of the most prominent figures in recent Ainu history. Born in Biratori, southern Hokkaido, not far from the capital Sapporo, he grew up speaking the Ainu language, only learning Japanese as an adult. Although lacking a formal education, he immersed himself in the history, culture and traditions of his people so thoroughly that he became one of the leading authorities on the subject. Above all, he played a crucial role in a court case that to this day remains one of the most important turning points in relations between the Japanese government and the Ainu. Having decided to build a dam on the Saru River, in the same region as Biratori, the Japanese expropriated land from indigenous farmers in the late 1980s.

To make matters worse, the dam was due to flood what the Ainu regarded as sacred territory. In response, Shigeru headed a protest that led to a long and historic court case, at the end of which the Ainu were unsuccessful in stopping the construction work on the dam (which was effectively completed in 1997) but obtained recognition of numerous fundamental rights, protected by Article 13 of the Japanese constitution, as an indigenous culture separate from and pre-dating that of the dominant Yamato culture. This act represented an admission on the part of Japan that the annexation of Hokkaido had to all intents and purposes been a colonial undertaking involving the oppression of the island's native people and helped to establish the conditions for a more benevolent approach towards the Ainu.

Above: Senke Morio, craftsman and former photographer.
Pages 94–5: A bear skull surrounded by *inao* prayer sticks (left) and a bear in a cage (right), both at the Poroto Kotan Museum in Shiraoi, Hokkaido.

It is a relationship that often has a more dramatic tone here than in other places, so much so that it suggests that the Hokkaido bear carries ancestral characteristics that can be explained only through myth. It can happen, as in June 2016, that a bear kills residents of the island, although such aggressive behaviour seldom occurs, even in areas like Alaska where the coexistence of man and this predator has many parallels with those in Hokkaido. The 2016 incident, in which four people were killed, was preceded by another in 2009 that left nine people injured and occurred more than a century after one of the most tragic events involving a bear recorded anywhere in the world. The Japanese know it as the *Sankebetsu higuma jiken* ('the Sankebetsu bear incident') or *Rokusensawa yūgai jiken* ('the Rokusensawa bear attack), and it took place between 9 and 14 December 1915, when a bear, just having woken after hibernation, attacked two Yamato colonial villages, Sankebetsu and Rokusensawa, that had recently been built. The events of those five days were reported hour by hour, attack by attack, and sound more like a horror story than a genuine historical occurrence.

According to reports, prey to a murderous fit never before witnessed in bears, this individual, named Kesagake by a local hunter who suspected it had already killed three women in a neighbouring village, came to Sankebetsu and Rokusensawa day after day, night after night, sowing panic and death. So much so that on the second day of the attack all the residents of both villages had to take shelter in a building protected by armed men while a patrol of hunters and police officers pursued the bear, by now considered a kind of supernatural scourge. Repeatedly shot, Kesagake was finally killed on the morning of 14 December by Yamamoto Heikichi, the area's most skilled hunter, remembered today as a local hero.

After Kesagake was skinned, the remains of its victims were found in its stomach. The bear weighed 340 kilos, unusually large for a Hokkaido specimen. Over five days of terror it had succeeded in killing seven people and injuring twelve. After the attack, the residents of Rokusensawa abandoned their village, and its ghostly remains can still be seen, although they are now covered in thick foliage.

There remains one old hut preserved in Sankebetsu, however. It belonged to the Ōta family, the first to be destroyed by the

A grocery-shop delivery man holding a bear paw taken as a hunting trophy.

animal. Next to it stands an unrealistically tall reproduction of a bear, its jaws open. It looks like a *kaijū*, a Godzilla-type monster, one of Japan's most successful pop exports. Resurrected after the war on the back of the emotional wave following the fear of the atom bomb, *kaijū* have a very ancient history rooted in the *Shan Hai Jing,* a Chinese bestiary dating from the fourth century BCE, which then became very popular in Japan. In a way, Kesagake has also become a legend in Japanese folklore, halfway between a child's fairy tale and a horror of the abyss. Just like Namazu, the catfish that controls the earthquakes. 🐾

Sea of Crises

A writer's journey to follow the most important tournament in the sumo calendar – with all its rituals and strict hierarchies – becomes a voyage into events buried in the past. Brian Phillips finds himself tracking a forgotten man, one who, in 1970, was involved in another ritual, a sensational case of seppuku, when he decapitated the writer Mishima Yukio following a failed coup d'état.

BRIAN PHILLIPS

A cut-out of a sumo wrestler outside the Kokugikan, Japan's national sumo stadium.

When he comes into the ring, Hakuhō, the greatest *sumōtori* in the world, perhaps the greatest in the history of the world, dances like a tropical bird, like a bird of paradise. Flanked by two attendants – his *tachimochi*, who carries his sword, and his *tsuyuharai*, or dew sweeper, who keeps the way clear for him – and wearing his embroidered apron, the *keshō-mawashi*, with its braided cords and intricate loops of rope, Hakuhō climbs on to the trapezoidal block of clay, sixty centimetres high and nearly seven metres across, where he will be fighting. Here, marked off by rice-straw bales, is the circle, the *dohyō*, which he has been trained to imagine as the top of a skyscraper: one step over the line and he is dead. A Shinto priest purified the *dohyō* before the tournament; above, a six-tonne canopy suspended from the arena's ceiling, a kind of floating temple roof, marks it as a sacred space. Coloured tassels hang from the canopy's corners, representing the Four Divine Beasts of the Chinese constellations: the azure dragon of the east, the vermilion sparrow of the south, the white tiger of the west, the black tortoise of the north. Over the canopy, off-centre and lit with spotlights, flies the white-and-red flag of Japan.

Hakuhō bends into a deep squat. He claps twice then rubs his hands together. He turns his palms slowly upwards. He is bare chested, 1.95 metres tall and weighs 158 kilograms. His hair is pulled up in a topknot. His smooth stomach strains against the coiled belt at his waist, the literal referent of his rank: *yokozuna*, horizontal rope. Rising, he lifts his right arm diagonally, palm down, to show he is unarmed. He repeats the gesture with his left. He lifts his right leg high into the air, tipping his torso to the left like a watering can, then slams his foot on to the clay. When it strikes, the crowd of thirteen thousand souls inside the Ryōgoku Kokugikan, Japan's national sumo stadium, shouts in unison: '*Yoisho!* – *Come on! Do it!*' He slams down his other foot: '*Yoisho!*' It's as if the force of his weight is striking the crowd in the stomach. Then he squats again, arms held out wing-like at his sides, and bends forward at the waist until his back is near parallel with the floor. Imagine someone playing aeroplanes with a small child. With weird, sliding thrusts of his feet, he inches forward, gliding across the ring's sand, raising and lowering his head in a way that's vaguely serpentine while slowly straightening his back. By the time he's upright again, the crowd is roaring.

*

Since 1749 sixty-nine men have been promoted to *yokozuna*. Only the holders of sumo's highest rank are allowed to make entrances like this. Officially, the purpose of the elaborate *dohyō-iri* is to chase away demons. (And this is something you should register about sumo, a sport with TV contracts and millions in revenue and fan blogs and athletes in yogurt commercials – that it's simultaneously a sport in which demon-frightening can be something's official purpose.) But the ceremony is territorial on a human level, too. It's a message delivered to adversaries, a way of

BRIAN PHILLIPS is an author and journalist with a passion for sport who works as a senior writer for MTV News. He has contributed to *Grantland*, *The New York Times*, *The New Republic* and *Slate*, as well as being included in the *Best American Sports Writing* and *Best American Magazine Writing* anthologies. This article is taken from his debut book *Impossible Owls*, a collection of narrative essays first published by FSG Originals in 2018. He lives in Los Angeles.

A cut-out of a sumo wrestler.

saying, *This ring is mine*; a way of saying, *Be prepared for what happens if you're crazy enough to enter it.*

Hakuhō is not Hakuhō's real name. Sumo wrestlers fight under ring names called *shikona*, formal pseudonyms governed, like everything else in sumo, by elaborate traditions and rules. Hakuhō was born Mönkhbatyn Davaajargal in Ulaanbaatar, Mongolia, in 1985; he is the fourth non-Japanese wrestler to attain *yokozuna* status. Until the last thirty years or so, foreigners were rare in the upper ranks of sumo in Japan. But some countries have their own sumo customs, brought over by immigrants, and others have sports that are very like sumo. Thomas Edison filmed sumo matches in Hawaii as early as 1903. Mongolian wrestling involves many of the same skills and concepts. In recent years wrestlers brought up in places such as these have found their way to Japan in greater numbers and have largely supplanted Japanese wrestlers at the top of the rankings. At the time of writing, six of the past eight *yokozuna* promotions have gone to foreigners, with no active Japanese *yokozuna* since the last retired in 2003. This is a source of intense anxiety to many in the tradition-minded world of sumo in Japan.

As a child, the story goes, Davaajargal was skinny. This was years before he became Hakuhō, when he used to mooch around Ulaanbaatar, thumbing through sumo magazines and fantasising about growing as big as a house. His father had been a dominant force in Mongolian wrestling in the 1960s and 1970s, winning a silver medal at the 1968 Olympics and rising to the rank of undefeatable giant. It was sumo that captured Davaajargal's imagination, but he was simply too small for it.

When he went to Tokyo, in October 2000, he was a 62-kilo fifteen-year-old. No trainer

Sea of Crises

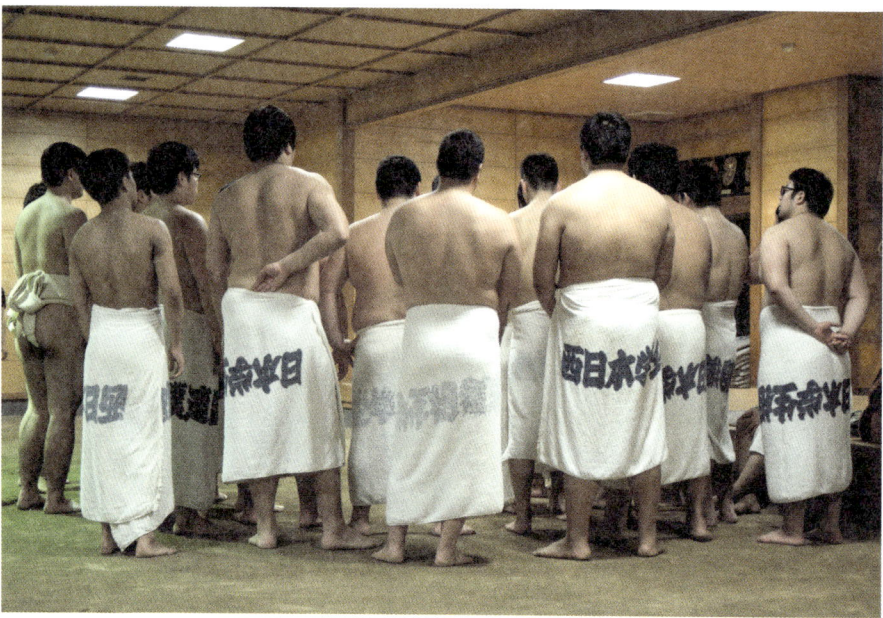

Top: A row of *mawashi*, the loincloths worn by sumo wrestlers, in the gym where members of the student sumo club train at Asahi University, Gifu Prefecture.
Bottom: Students gathered around their trainer before daily practice.

> '**Sumo apprentices start young, moving into training stables where they're given room and board in return for a life of eating, chores, training, eating and serving as quasi-slaves to their senior stablemates (and eating).**'

would touch him. Sumo apprentices start young, moving into training stables called *heya* where they're given room and board in return for a somewhat horrifying life of eating, chores, training, eating and serving as quasi-slaves to their senior stablemates (and eating). Everyone agreed that little Davaajargal had a stellar wrestling brain, but he was starting too late, and his reed-like body would make real wrestlers want to kick *dohyō* sand in his face. Finally, an expat Mongolian *rikishi* (another word for sumo wrestler) persuaded the master of the Miyagino *heya* to take Davaajargal in on the last day of the teenager's stay in Japan. The stablemaster's gamble paid off. After a few years of training and a fortuitous late growth spurt, Davaajargal emerged as the most feared young *rikishi* in Japan. He was given the name Hakuhō, which means White Peng (a Peng being a giant bird in Chinese mythology).

Hakuhō's early career was marked by a sometimes bad-tempered rivalry with an older wrestler, a fellow Mongolian called Asashōryū (Morning Blue Dragon), who became a *yokozuna* in 2003. Asashōryū embodied everything the Japanese fear about the wave of foreign *rikishi* who now dominate the sport. He was hot headed, unpredictable and indifferent to the ancient traditions of a sport that's been part of the Japanese national consciousness for as long as there's been a Japan.

This is something else you should register about sumo: it is very, very old. Not old like black-and-white movies; old like the mists of time. Sumo was already ancient when the current ranking system came into being in the mid-1700s. The artistry of the *banzuke*, the traditional ranking sheet, has given rise to an entire school of calligraphy.

Asashōryū brawled with other wrestlers in the communal baths. He barked at referees – an almost unthinkable offence. He pulled another wrestler's hair, a breach that made him the first *yokozuna* ever to be disqualified from a match. *Rikishi* are expected to wear kimonos and sandals in public; Asashōryū would show up in a business suit. He would show up drunk. He would accept his prize money with the wrong hand.

The 287-kilo Hawaiian *sumōtori* Konishiki launched a rap career after retiring from the sport; another Hawaiian, Akebono, the first foreign *yokozuna*, became a professional wrestler. This was bad enough. But Asashōryū flouted the dignity of the sumo association while still an active *rikishi*. He withdrew from a summer tour claiming an injury, then showed up on Mongolian TV playing in a charity soccer match. When sumo was rocked by a massive match-fixing scandal in the mid-2000s, a tabloid magazine reported that Asashōryū had paid his opponents US$10,000 per match to let him win one tournament. Along with several other wrestlers, Asashōryū won a settlement against the magazine, but even that victory carried a faint whiff of scandal: the Mongolian became the first *yokozuna* ever to appear in court. 'Everyone talks about dignity,' Asashōryū complained when he retired, 'but when I went into the ring I felt fierce like a devil.' Once, after an especially contentious bout, he reportedly went into the car park and attacked his adversary's car.

The problem, from the perspective of the traditionalists who control Japanese sumo, was that Asashōryū also won. He won relentlessly. He laid waste to the sport. Until Hakuhō came along he was, by an enormous margin, the best wrestler in the world. The sumo calendar revolves around six grand tournaments – *honbasho* – held every two months throughout the year. In 2004 Asashōryū won five of them, two with perfect 15-0 records, a mark that no one had achieved since the mid-1990s. In 2005 he became the first wrestler to win all six *honbasho* in a single year. He would lift 180-kilogram wrestlers off their feet and hurl them, writhing, to the clay. He would bludgeon them with hands toughened by countless hours of striking the *teppō*, a wooden shaft as thick as a telephone pole. He won his twenty-fifth tournament, then good for third on the all-time list, before his thirtieth birthday.

Hakuhō began to make waves around the peak of Asashōryū's invulnerable reign. Five years younger than his rival, Hakuhō was temperamentally his opposite: solemn, silent, difficult to read. 'More Japanese than the Japanese' – this is what people say about him. Asashōryū made sumo look wild and furious; Hakuhō was fathomlessly calm. He seemed to have an innate sense of angles and counterweights, how to shift his hips almost imperceptibly to annihilate his enemy's balance. In concept, winning a sumo bout is simple: either make your opponent step outside the ring or make him touch the ground with any part of his body besides the soles of his feet. When Hakuhō won, how he'd done it was sometimes a mystery. The other wrestler would go staggering out of what looked like an even grapple. When Hakuhō needed to, he could be overpowering. He didn't often need to.

The flaming circus of Asashōryū's career was good for TV ratings. But Hakuhō was a way forward for a scandal-torn sport – a foreign *rikishi* with deep feelings for Japanese tradition, a figure who could unite the past and future. At first he lost to Asashōryū more than he won, but the rivalry always ran hot. In 2008, almost exactly a year after the Yokozuna Deliberation Council promoted Hakuhō to the top rank, Asashōryū gave him an extra shove after hurling him down in a tournament. The two momentarily squared off. In the video of the bout you can see the older man grinning and shaking his head while Hakuhō glares at him with an air of outraged grace. Over time Hakuhō's fearsome technique and Asashōryū's endless seesawing between injury and controversy turned the tide in the younger wrestler's favour. When Asashōryū retired unexpectedly in 2010 after allegedly breaking a man's nose outside a nightclub, Hakuhō had taken their last seven regulation matches and notched a 14-13 lifetime record against his formerly invincible adversary.

With no Asashōryū to contend with, Hakuhō proceeded to go 15-0 in his next four tournaments. He began a spell of dominance that not even Asashōryū could have matched. In 2010 he compiled the second-longest winning streak in sumo history, sixty-three straight wins, which tied a record set in the 1780s. By 2014 he had won a record ten tournaments without dropping a single match.

*

Watching Hakuhō's ring entrance, that harrowing bird dance, it is hard to imagine what his life is like. To have doubled in

Students hang up their *mawashi* at the end of a training session.

size, more than doubled, in the years since his fifteenth birthday; to have jumped cultures and languages; to have unlocked this arcane expertise. To be followed on the street. To be a non-Japanese acting as a samurai incarnate, the last remnant of a fading culture. When I landed in Tokyo there was one other *yokozuna* in Japan, Harumafuji, another Mongolian. He was widely seen as a second-tier champion, and when I arrived he was out with an ankle injury. Hakuhō is everything. How do you experience that without losing all sense of identity? How do you remember who you are?

But it's time, here at the Kokugikan, for his first match of the *hatsu basho*, the first grand tournament of the year. *Rikishi* in sumo's top division wrestle once per day during the fifteen-day derby; whoever has the best record at the end of the final day wins the Emperor's Cup. Hakuhō opens against Tochiōzan, a Japanese *komusubi* – the fourth rank, three tiers below *yokozuna*. Tochiōzan is known for outmuscling his opponents by gripping their loincloth, the *mawashi*. The wrestlers squat at their marks. The referee stands between them in shining purple robes holding his war fan up. The crowd calls Hakuhō's name. There's a roar as the fighters lunge for one another. Nothing Hakuhō does looks difficult. He spins slightly out of the way as Tochiōzan grabs, unsuccessfully, for his *mawashi*. Then he uses his rotation as a wind-up to smash the other wrestler in the chest. Tochiōzan staggers back, and Hakuhō presses the advantage – one shove, two, three and now Tochiōzan is over the barrier, the referee pointing his war fan toward Hakuhō's side to indicate victory. The entire match lasts four seconds.

He doesn't celebrate. He returns to his mark, bows to Tochiōzan and squats as the

Left and page 109: Giant photographs of sumo wrestlers on display at the station in Ryōgoku, the sumo district, which, in addition to the Kokugikan, is also home to various *heya*, the sumo stables where the *rikishi* live and train.

referee again points to him with the fan. Win or lose, sumo wrestlers are forbidden from betraying emotion. That was the sin Asashōryū used to commit; he'd raise a fist after winning or snarl a happy snarl. Hakuhō is not so careless. Hakuhō is discreet. There are many crimes a *sumōtori* can commit. The worst is revealing too much.

Some Japanese stories end violently. Others never end at all but only cut away, at the moment of extreme crisis, to a butterfly or the wind or the moon. This is true of stories everywhere, of course: their endings can be abrupt or oblique. But in Japan, where suicide is historically woven into the culture, where an awareness of life's evanescence is the traditional mode of aesthetics, it seems truer than in other places.

For instance, in January 2014 I flew to Tokyo to spend two weeks watching sumo wrestling. Tokyo, the city where my parents were married – I remember gazing up at their Japanese wedding certificate on the wall and wondering what it meant. Tokyo, the biggest city in the world, the biggest city in the history of the world, a galaxy reflected in its own glass. It was a fishing village barely four hundred years ago, and now, 37 million people, a human concourse so vast it can't be said to *end*, only to fade indeterminately around the edges; 37 million, almost the population of California. Smells mauling you from doorways: stale beer, steaming broth, char-grilled eel. Intersections where a thousand people cross each time the light changes, under J-pop videos ten storeys tall. Flocks of schoolgirls in blue blazers and plaid skirts. Boys with frosted tips and oversize headphones, camouflage jackets and cashmere scarves. Herds of black-suited businessmen. A city so dense the 24-hour manga cafés will rent you a pod to sleep in for the night, so post-human there are brothels where the prostitutes are dolls. An unnavigable labyrinth with 1,900 kilometres of railway, a thousand train stations, homes with no addresses, restaurants with no names. Endless warrens of *Blade Runner* alleys where paper lanterns float among criss-crossing power lines. And yet: clean, safe, quiet, somehow weightless, a place whose order seems sustained by the logic of a dream.

It's a dream city, Tokyo. I mean that literally, in that I often felt like I was experiencing it while asleep. You'll ride an escalator underground into what your map says is a tunnel between metro stops only to find yourself in a thumping subterranean mall packed with beautiful teenagers dancing to Katy Perry remixes. You will take a turn off a busy street and into a deserted Buddhist graveyard, soundless but for the wind and the clacking of *sotōba* sticks, wooden markers crowded with the names of the dead. You will stand in a high tower and look out on the reason-defying extent of the city, windows and David Beckham billboards and aerial expressways falling lightly downwards towards the Ferris wheel on the edge of the sea.

Part of this had to do with another Japanese story, one I found myself increasingly preoccupied with, even though it had nothing to do with the wrestling culture I'd come to Japan to observe. This story fitted into mine – or maybe vice versa – like the nesting sumo dolls I saw one afternoon in a *chanko* shop window

Sea of Crises

> 'As a child Mishima had been sickly and sheltered. Now he worshipped samurai and scorned the idea of peace. He fantasised about dying for the emperor, dying horribly.'

(*chanko*: the weight-gaining stew eaten in huge quantities by *sumōtori*), the smaller fighters enclosed in the larger, tortoises in a strange shell. It was a distraction, but, unlike almost everything else during those weeks, I couldn't get it out of my mind.

*

On the flight to Tokyo I brought a novel by Mishima Yukio. *Runaway Horses*, first issued in 1969 (published by Vintage in English), is the second book in his *Sea of Fertility* tetralogy, which was the last work he completed before his spectacular suicide in 1970. What happened was that he sat down on the floor and ran a dagger through his abdomen, spilling fifty centimetres of intestine in front of the general whom he had just kidnapped, bound and gagged. He had taken the general hostage in his own office in the headquarters of the Japan Self-Defense Forces (SDF) in a failed attempt to overthrow the government. If you tour the building today you can see the gouges the writer's sword left in the doorframe when he fought off the general's aides.

Mishima was a contradiction. Handsome, rich, a perennial contender for the Nobel Prize, he was, at forty-five, a national celebrity, one of the most famous men in the country. He was also possessed by an increasingly charismatic and death-obsessed vision of Japanese culture. After its defeat in the Second World War, Japan had accepted severe constraints on its military, had turned away from martial values. The SDF was the shadow of an army, not really an army at all. Mishima not only rejected these changes but found them impossible to bear. As a child he had been sickly and sheltered. Now he worshipped samurai and scorned the idea of peace. He fantasised about dying for the emperor, dying horribly: he posed in an artist's photo shoot as the martyred St Sebastian, his arms bound to a tree, arrows protruding from his sides.

In 1968, horrified by the scale of left-wing protests in Tokyo, Mishima founded a private army, the Tatenokai, advertising for soldiers in right-wing student newspapers. A married father, he had long haunted Tokyo gay bars. He fell in love with the Tatenokai's second-in-command, a young man called Morita Masakatsu, and began to imagine a coup attempt that would double as a kind of erotic transfiguration, an all-consuming climax of the sort that sometimes fell at the end of kabuki melodramas.

And so, in 1970 Mishima made an appointment to visit the headquarters of the SDF accompanied by four young Tatenokai officers. He wore his brown Tatenokai uniform, sword in a scabbard at his belt. When the general asked to see the blade, a seventeenth-century weapon forged by the Seki no Magoroku line of swordsmiths, the writer requested a handkerchief to clean it. This was the signal for the four Tatenokai officers to seize the general and barricade the door.

Here is what I see when I picture this scene: the orange tassel hanging from the hilt of Mishima's sword; the twin rows of metallic buttons on the brown tunics of the

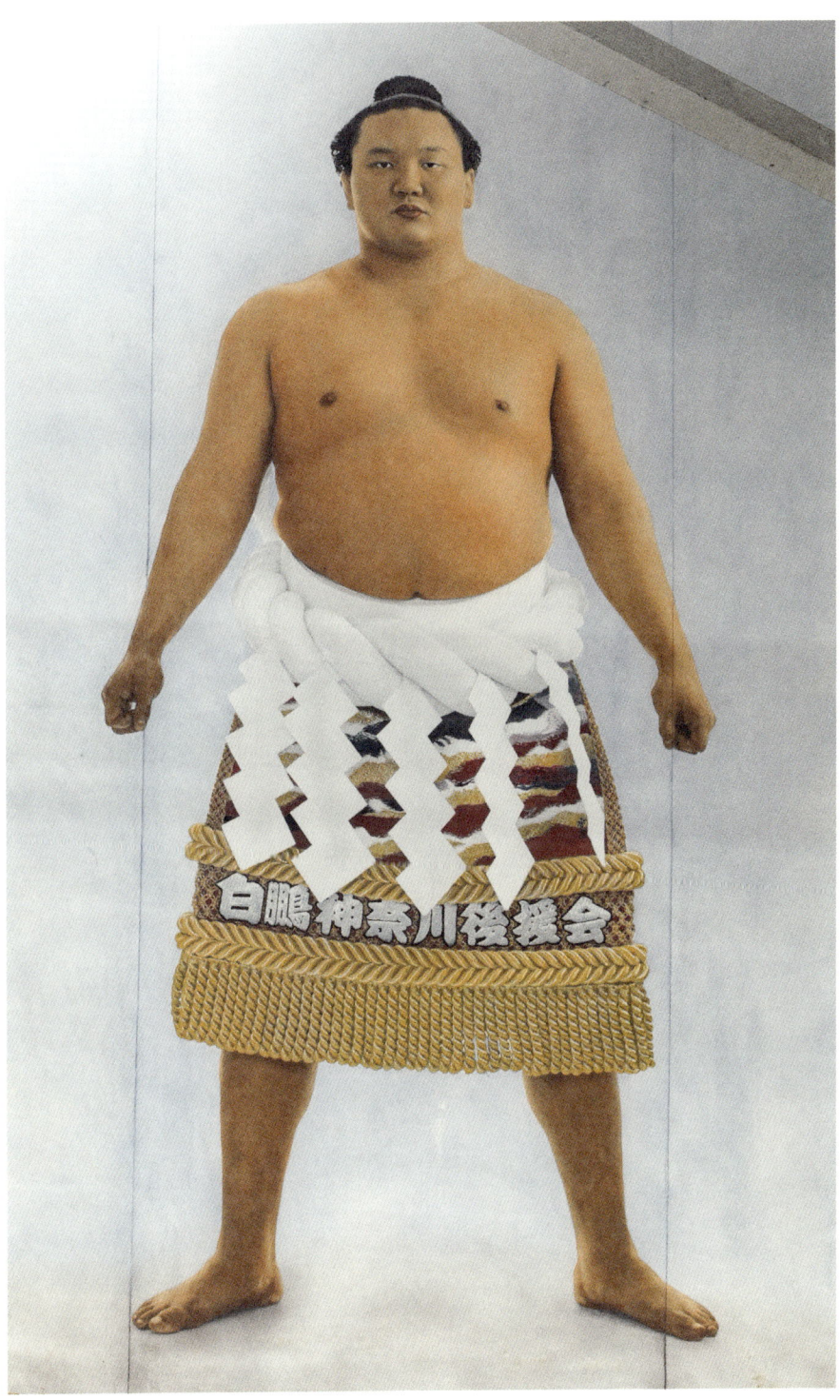

Sea of Crises

A sumo wrestler waiting for a taxi.

Tatenokai officers; the polite smile on the general's face in the moment before he felt himself grabbed from behind.

Mishima went on to the general's balcony and delivered a fiery speech to the soldiers, around a thousand of them, assembled below. He urged the members of the SDF to take their place as a true national army, as warriors devoted to the emperor – a move that, had it succeeded, would have shattered the social structure of post-war Japan. He was asking the men to stage a coup. The soldiers jeered him. There is broad consensus among scholars that Mishima never expected the coup to succeed, that his only aim was to die gloriously. But he had planned to speak for half an hour, and he gave up after seven minutes. 'I don't think they even heard me,' he said as he climbed in through the window. Back in the general's office he unbuttoned his uniform jacket. The young officers could hear helicopters circling outside, police sirens wailing. Mishima sat down. He screamed. Then he drove the dagger with both hands into his stomach.

Here is what I think about when I envision this scene: the moment earlier that morning when the Tatenokai officers, none older than twenty-five, stopped to wash their car on the way to Mishima's house; Mishima joking on the drive about what sort of music would play in a yakuza movie at that moment (he began to sing a song from the 1966 gangster flick *Karajishi botan* [*A Lion Amid Peonies*]; the younger men joined in); the gagged general's eyes bulging as one of Japan's most celebrated writers committed seppuku on his floor.

'Please,' Mishima gasped, 'do not leave me in agony too long.' He was speaking to his lover, Morita, the student leader of the Tatenokai, whose role in the ritual was to cut off Mishima's head. In a formal seppuku, the *kaishakunin* decapitates the dying man, sparing him the prolonged anguish of death by disembowelment. Morita hacked at Mishima's neck but missed, slicing into his shoulder. He tried again and left a wound across his back. A third stroke cut into the neck but not deeply enough. Finally, another Tatenokai officer, a law student named Koga Hiroyasu, took the sword from Morita – the writer's sword, the sword with the orange tassel – and beheaded Mishima in one blow.

Morita, as planned, then kneeled and tried to commit seppuku. He was too weak. At his signal, Koga beheaded him, too.

In the confusion afterwards, as Koga and the other officers surrendered, as reporters struggled to piece together the sequence of events, Mishima's sword was taken into custody by police. Some time later it went missing.

Here is what I wonder when I try to imagine this scene: *What did this feel like for Koga?* To have followed Mishima into that place and then, unexpectedly, to have been called on to cut off his head? To have lived the rest of his life with that memory? Koga, too, was prepared to commit seppuku – all the young men were – but, shortly before the coup attempt, Mishima ordered them to live, charging them to explain his actions to the world. To have drifted out of the centre of the story, drifted into obscurity, carrying those moments with him? At his trial, where he was sentenced to four years in prison for (among other things) 'murder by agreement', Koga said that to live as a Japanese is to live the history of Japan, that the experience of each Japanese person is the experience of the nation in microcosm. What a history he must have conceived, I thought, to have said that, having done what he had.

On my third day in Tokyo I discovered that he was alive.

Sea of Crises

THE FLOATING WORLD

Watch the slow, sad figure of the *yobidashi* with his broom, endlessly sweeping the edges of the ring. For the long minutes between bouts, while the wrestlers move through their preparations, this slight man circles gravely and patiently, smoothing sand, erasing footprints. No mark can be allowed beyond the line because the judges must be able to tell at a glance whether a toe has landed outside the *dohyō*, whether a heel has slipped. Each *rikishi* is called into the ring by a singer, then announced over the stadium loudspeakers by a voice that sounds strangled and furious, like an oboe filtered through the dive alarm on a submarine. Through this, the *yobidashi* sweeps.

The wrestlers face off at their marks, not once but twice, three times, squatting and flexing, glaring intimidation at each other. Then they break and walk to their corners, where they scoop salt out of a bowl and hurl it across the clay – another Shinto purification ritual. The *yobidashi* sweeps the salt, mixing it into the sand. Tall silk banners representing sponsors' bonus prizes – extra money guaranteed for the winner of the bout – are carried around the ring on poles. The *yobidashi* sweeps around the banners. The wrestlers slap their bellies, slap their thighs, signalling massiveness to their enemies. The spectators, who know the routine, chat lightly, snap pictures, reach out to receive bags of snacks from the tea-shop waiters who circulate through the aisles. At the centre of the ring the referee poses and flits his fan, a luminary in silks; the hilt of his knife, which he wears as a reminder of the days when one wrong decision meant his immediate seppuku, peeks out from the sash at his waist. Through all this, the *yobidashi* sweeps.

Then the atmosphere changes. The

JAPAN SELF-DEFENSE FORCES

The pacifist constitution passed in 1946 after Japan's defeat in the Second World War denied the country the right to go to war or to have an army. The intent of the measures dictated by the USA was to rid Japanese society of its militarism once and for all, but the intensity of the Cold War made a partial revision necessary just a few years later, leading in 1954 to the creation of the Japan Self-Defense Forces (SDF), which were to assist and share the burden of the US military. Although they have always been a *de facto* army – the eighth-largest in the world in terms of budget, with a cutting-edge navy considered superior to its Chinese counterpart – they have no offensive weapons such as bombers, aircraft carriers or long-range ballistic missiles and have long been seen as a sort of civil protection force that intervenes in the event of natural disasters and internal emergencies. After the end of the Cold War the SDF were also involved in international peacekeeping missions – in Iraq, for example. In 2005 the Abe government approved a controversial law, which many see as unconstitutional, introducing the concept of 'collective self-defence' and extending the remit of Japan's military beyond its borders.

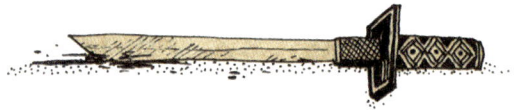

crowd grows quiet. The *rikishi* toss one last handful of salt and stamp back to their marks, fat torsos shining. The referee's fan hangs in the air between them. And in the last split second before the combatants launch at one another, the *yobidashi*, who has never changed his pace, who has never at any point moved without perfect deliberation and slow, sad care, lifts his broom and steps down from the *dohyō*.

And here is something you should register about sumo: how intensely hierarchical it is. It is not only the *sumōtori* who are ranked. Referees are ranked, too. So are *yobidashi*.

Hakuhō glides through his first five matches. On Day Two he lets the diminutive and root-vegetable-like Toyonoshima – 1.68 metres tall and maybe 1.73 from rump to navel – push him almost to the edge of the ring, only then, when Toyonoshima lunges in with what looks like the winning shove, Hakuhō just *isn't there*; Toyonoshima does an arms-flailing slapstick belly flop over the line. On Day Three Hakuhō gets a grip on the *mawashi* of Okinoumi, a wrestler known for his movie-star looks. Okinoumi outweighs the *yokozuna* by nine kilograms, but Hakuhō lifts him half off the clay and guides him out of the ring; it's like watching someone move an end table. On Day Four, against Chiyotairyū, a wrestler whose leg he once snapped in a match, Hakuhō slams his adversary with the first charge then skips aside; Chiyotairyū drops; the bout lasts one second. On Day Five he grapples with Ikioi, a physically strong wrestler known for controlling his opponent's *mawashi*. Hakuhō ducks out of Ikioi's grasp, plants a hand on the back of his adversary's neck and thrusts him to the floor. It takes a sumo novice perhaps ten seconds of match action to see that among the top-class *rikishi* Hakuhō occupies a category of his own. What the others are doing in the ring is fighting. Hakuhō is composing little haiku of battle.

There is a feeling of trepidation in the crowd over these first five days because the Yokozuna Deliberation Council has come to the stadium to observe Kisenosato, a wrestler of the second rank, *ōzeki*, who is being considered for promotion. This is a rare event. Unlike a *sumōtori* of any other rank, a *yokozuna* can never be demoted, only pressured to retire, so the council must make its recommendation with great care. It has fifty members, all sumo outsiders, professors and playwrights, dark-suited dignitaries from various backgrounds. For five days they tilt their heads back and scrutinise the action. They are austere and haughty, their lips as shrivelled as fried bacon. The crowd is anxious because Kisenosato is Japanese, his country's best hope for a native-born *yokozuna*, and he has already failed in one promotion attempt.

The hope of Japan is sour faced and prim, a 1.88-metre, 156-kilogram maiden aunt in a crimson loincloth. His stomach protrudes inflexibly straight in front of him; his soft breasts hang to either side. When he enters the *dohyō* his posture is erect. When he swings his arms before the fight, he does so with a strange, balletic slowness. On the first day, with the council looking on, he wrestles Toyonoshima, the root vegetable.

The crowd is afraid because Kisenosato is thought to be weak under pressure. The smack as their bellies collide is thunderous. Toyonoshima drives his stubby legs into the clay, trying to force Kisenosato backwards. Kisenosato gets a right-handed grip on Toyonoshima's pale-green *mawashi*, but he fails to lift Toyonoshima, his hand slips off and his fallback attempt to throw his opponent also fails. Now he is in trouble. Toyonoshima is a little locomotive, churning forward. The wrestlers' guts grind together. Muscles leap in their thighs. With a huge effort, Kisenosato grunts his way back to the centre of the *dohyō*, gets Toyonoshima in check. Toyonoshima twists his torso hard to divert the larger man's momentum, and the throw works; Kisenosato's knee folds, and he goes over on to his back then rolls over the edge of the clay platform and into the photographers' trench. He rests on his hands and knees, defeated, surrounded by flashbulbs.

On the fifth day Kisenosato goes over the edge again, this time battered out by the frenzied shoves of Aoiyama, a gigantic Bulgarian. The frowns of the Yokozuna Deliberation Council go right to the pit of your stomach. There is talk later that Kisenosato has suffered a toe injury. Regardless, he will lose more than he wins at the *hatsu basho*, finishing 7-8, falling to Hakuhō on Day Thirteen, and there will be no Japanese *yokozuna* this time in the sport that most embodies the history of Japan.

*

I thought about Koga Hiroyasu.

As of 2005, I learned from Wikipedia, Koga was a practising Shinto priest on Shikoku, the smallest of Japan's main islands. I pictured him in his white robes, standing in a cemetery behind a dark gate.

The way you remember things in a dream is not precisely like remembering, yet anything you've experienced can come back to you in a dream. Under the shoguns, sumo wrestlers often appeared in *ukiyo-e* – meaning 'pictures of the floating world' – woodblock prints from the pleasure districts whose other great subjects were courtesans and kabuki actors, musicians and fishermen, archers and demons and ghosts. I went to an *ukiyo-e* exhibition and noted the wrestlers intermixed among the geisha, among the snarling samurai. Their bellies were rendered with one or two curved brushstrokes, their navels cartoon Xs. Their eyes were oddly placid, and I thought: It will be a miracle if I can ever finish a thought.

And I thought about Koga. I'm not sure why. I didn't know how I'd find him. I didn't know how I'd speak to him. But I priced tickets to Shikoku. I looked at the sumo schedule to figure out when I could get away. To be honest, Mishima's suicide had always struck me as somewhat absurd – in bad taste, at the very least. But I thought: It is a small island. If I can get to the train station I can walk to the shrine, and I will find him there.

Then I looked at a map of Shikoku. 'The smallest of Japan's main islands' covers nineteen thousand square kilometres, is home to 4.1 million people and contains dozens of Shinto shrines. I gave up.

But I found that I couldn't give up. Whenever I stepped on to a metro train, whenever I rode an escalator up into the light, the idea came back, and I thought: If I can track down the shrine I will find him there. I tried to locate a directory of Shinto sites on Shikoku – but how to make contact with one, how to ask for him?

Hello, yes, are you familiar with this celebrated author? Wonderful. Now, did one of your priests by any chance decapitate him in the early 1970s using a 400-year-old samurai sword that has since vanished?

It was an impossible question to imagine putting in English much less Japanese. And I spoke no Japanese. I pictured the look on the face of whomever I roped into being my interpreter.

Finally, I wrote an email to my friend Alex, a college professor who studies Japanese literature and film. 'Weird Japan question' was the subject line. I asked if he had any thoughts about how I could track down Mishima's *kaishakunin*. I hit send. And I waited for an answer, wandering

Students at the Asahi University sumo club sweep the *dohyō*, the sacred wrestling ring, before training.

Sea of Crises

Below and pages 119 and 120:
Two students at the Asahi University sumo club fight during a training session.

SEPPUKU

The samurai practice of ritual suicide dates back to the twelfth century and involves disembowelment with a dagger to free the soul and accept an honourable death to atone for shame or guilt or in order not to give in to an enemy. This last course of action was often taken during the Second World War, both among regular soldiers and high-ranking army officers – the ultra-nationalist General Chō and General Ushijima Mitsuru, both of whom were Japanese commanders during the Battle of Okinawa (1945), were two such. When the news of Mishima Yukio's suicide broke, there had been no public cases of seppuku since the war, and the incredulous newspaper editors thought their journalists had misunderstood. The evening edition of one newspaper ran with the headline: 'Mishima Wounded and Rushed to Hospital'. There was also a less cruel ritual for female suicide, known as *jigai*, undertaken by cutting veins. In 2001 a further case of seppuku took place when the judoka Inokuma Isao, who had won a gold medal at the 1964 Olympics, took his own life because of financial difficulties.

through the city, lost. I listened to jazz in blue doorways. I pulled my coat a little tighter. I watched the setting sun float in pale high glass.

THE MANDARIN DUCKS

In the Kokugikan there are stories of ghosts, sounds with no sources, invisible hands that seize you from behind. Security guards are reluctant to enter a certain hallway at night. A reporter from the *Asahi Shimbun* recalls being shoved in the back by something large and round 'like a volleyball' only to turn and find that 'no one was there'. A clerk is pulled from behind while using a urinal. The clatter of sumo practice comes from an empty dressing room. Somewhere under or near the stadium is said to be a mass grave containing victims of the great fire of 1657, which razed two-thirds of Tokyo and killed a hundred thousand. The shogun built a temple to commemorate the dead; the temple became the site of sumo matches whose popularity led to the construction of the first national arena in 1909.

Even to die in this country, you might say to yourself, is somehow to live the history of Japan. But this thought does not seem to weigh on the fans streaming through the gates under banners of watery silk, nor on the *gaijin* (foreign) tourists lined up in the entrance hall to buy the little glitchy radios that offer audio commentary in English. The tourists talk about being tourists and about the ¥1,000 deposit for the radios. Is it refundable or not? It is refundable. No one talks about ghosts.

Hakuhō is frictionless, devastating. He wins his next eight matches. On Day Ten Hakuhō hits his fellow Mongolian, the 39-year-old Kyokutenhō, so hard that the older man practically rolls out of the ring. On Day Thirteen he wrestles Kisenosato, the Japanese *rikishi* who has flubbed his chance to be promoted to *yokozuna* and is fighting only for pride. The match is furious, Hakuhō thrusting his open hand repeatedly into Kisenosato's neck; neither man can get a grip on the other's *mawashi*, so they simply bash one another, tactically berserk. Little violent nasal exhalations, the sound of a spray bottle's trigger being squeezed. Finally, with his foot braced on the edge of the rice-bale circle, Kisenosato twists to throw Hakuhō and fails. The *yokozuna* loses his balance and lurches forward but Kisenosato also stumbles backwards; Kisenosato's foot touches out of bounds a fraction of a second before Hakuhō's hand. The *yobidashi* sweeps up the marks.

On Day Fourteen Hakuhō wrestles Kotoshōgiku, an *ōzeki* from Fukuoka who specialises in bodying his opponents with his torso. Kotoshōgiku seems to have grappled Hakuhō to a standstill, the two men bent at the hips and clinging to one another in the middle of the *dohyō*, and then Hakuhō slaps his left hand against Kotoshōgiku's knee. Kotoshōgiku crumples; the move is so unexpected and counter-intuitive – and the end so sudden – that the match almost looks fixed. Hakuhō shows no emotion. On the second-to-last day of the tournament he is 14-0 and one win away from a perfect championship – a *zenshō yūshō*.

His body is strange, Hakuhō's. It's smooth, almost unformed, neither muscled like a boxer's nor bloated like that of many *rikishi*. Gagamaru, the Georgian wrestler who is currently the largest man in top-division sumo – two hundred kilograms and a little over 1.83 metres tall – looks like a canyon seen from the air, all crevasses and folds. Hakuhō, in contrast, is a single large stone. His face is vague, broad, so that his eyes look small and rimless, but also inexpressive, self-contained. Once in a while he will glance to one side with what looks like critical intelligence. Then he blurs again. The sources of his strength, whether physical or psychological, are almost totally hidden from view.

Another Mongolian, the *ōzeki* Kakuryū, has fought his way to a 13-1 record, making him the only *rikishi* with a chance to tie Hakuhō and force a play-off. Kakuryū is the son of a university professor who, unlike Hakuhō's father, had no background in Mongolian wrestling. With the championship at stake, he and Hakuhō are scheduled to meet on the tournament's final day.

*

'Re: Weird Japan question' dinged into my inbox in the middle of the night. 'Sounds like a cool piece,' Alex wrote. He had looked into the Koga question, and, as far as he could tell, Shikoku was a red herring. Koga had never lived there. Nor was he a Shinto priest. He had indeed joined a religious group, but it was Seichō no Ie, the House of Growth, a spiritual movement founded in the 1930s. Seichō no Ie fuses Christianity with Buddhism and Shintoism. After prison Koga became the head of its branch in Hokkaido, the snowy island in northern Japan where he had been born and raised. He married the daughter of the group's leader and changed his name to reflect that he'd been adopted into her family: Arechi Hiroyasu. Arechi was an unusual Japanese name, formed from characters that meant wild land or barren ground. 'If you want to get really literary,' Alex told me, 'Arechi' was also a Japanese translation of the title of T.S. Eliot's poem 'The Waste Land'. But that was only a coincidence.

Seichō no Ie struck a chord, so I looked it up in one of the Mishima biographies. There it was: the writer's grandmother had been a member. When Koga said at his trial that to live as a Japanese is to live the history of Japan, he was quoting one of the group's teachings.

Then Alex sent me a link that made me cover my mouth with my hand. Koga/Arechi retired in 2012 and moved to the other end of the country, to the city of Kumamoto on the southern island of Kyushu. The link led to a video from the website of an apartment complex in Kumamoto. In it, a 65-year-old man named Arechi Hiroyasu answers questions about being a new resident. He mentions at the beginning that he is from Hokkaido. He wears a black V-neck sweater over a red-and-white gingham sports shirt. His features match those of the young Koga in a photograph I'd seen of him posing with fellow Tatenokai conspirators, looking fierce in their ridiculous *faux*-military uniforms.

The older man in the video has warm eyes. As he speaks, we see a bit of his apartment in the background. Flowers hanging on a light-flooded balcony. A cream-coloured curtain tied back. An inset picture on the website shows a console table that holds framed photographs of what look like children and grandchildren. A couple holding hands in front of a landscape. Young people at a wedding. A man or woman in a parka, smiling, surrounded by snow.

He does not mention decapitation or suicide or Mishima. He says that the bus stop is very convenient for the building. The sales representatives are compassionate and polite. The park nearby is a good place to take walks. There is a MaxValu store across the street, open twenty-four hours, a handy place to shop. There is a roof garden. He has a wide balcony. There are beautiful views at night.

*

I remember the auditorium of the Kabuki-za theatre, warm and high and tinted by lights reflecting off the lavish pictorial curtains – herons in a stream, Mount Fuji, a hummingbird breaking

'Then the lovers' costumes turned inside out, revealing brilliant plumage, plumage like an illustration in a children's book, feathers as vivid as fire. Then they all froze in place, and the curtain dropped.'

out of a tangle of cherry blossoms. Tiny old ladies in surgical masks sat with *bentō* boxes resting on their knees, looking pleased; packs of theatre kids sprawled in fishnet tights. Old men slept in their chairs with both hands balanced on their canes. The kabuki play I had come to see was about sumo or involved sumo; I was not entirely sure. The English-language audio guide I had rented was unclear about the details. The play's story was fantastically complex and was itself only a tiny peripheral fragment of a larger story about two brothers seeking revenge for the murder of their father, a revenge that spanned decades and flowed inexorably from an equally long back story. The story when the curtain opened, however, was simple. It was a story about love.

A beautiful young woman was adored by two men. She herself loved the handsome youth with the impossibly sad white face, but the burly cross-eyed villain with the orange-red face was determined to win her hand. The villain (I learned from the voice in my ear) had never lost a sumo match. So the youth with the sad white face and the wrestler with the orange-red face wrestled to decide who would marry the woman. They danced this, spinning slowly and not quite touching their hands. At last the youth with the sad white face won the match. But the cross-eyed villain explained in an evil aside to the audience that he would yet betray the lovers. Spotting a pair of mandarin ducks on the lake, he threw his dagger and killed the male (a little wooden duck turned upside down, like a prop in a carnival). The villain explained that if he could trick the youth into drinking the duck's blood it would drive him mad. And he did so.

But the mandarin duck is a symbol of marriage, of fidelity, and now, in some mystical way, the two young lovers began to swirl. They swirled until they became the ducks. They became, by magic, the souls of the ducks. They took to the air on bright wings. They had become transcendent, timeless. On the same ground where the sumo match was fought, the duck-souls attacked the wrestler. They danced this, darting and bending their backs. The ducks drove the cross-eyed villain to the ground, making him even more cross-eyed. Then the lovers' costumes turned inside out, revealing brilliant plumage, plumage like an illustration in a children's book, feathers as vivid as fire. Then they all froze in place, and the curtain dropped.

THE RECONSTRUCTED CASTLE

Mishima's novel *Runaway Horses* tells, in part, the story of a samurai rebellion. In 1868 the reign of the shoguns ended and power reverted to the emperor of Japan or (because nothing is ever as simple as the official story) to a group of powerful men acting in his name. One of the consequences of this event, which is called the Meiji Restoration, was that the large samurai class that had governed Japan for hundreds of years was stripped of its power and dissolved. Imperial edicts forced members of the former warrior caste to stop styling their hair in topknots, to stop carrying swords. The twentieth-century Western idea of the samurai as an armoured warrior, a kind of Japanese knight, is not particularly accurate. Some samurai were warriors, and samurai were licensed to carry swords. But by the nineteenth century the samurai class had evolved into a kind of hereditary government bureaucracy. Many were officials whose roles had nothing to do with war.

In 1876 a group of two hundred reactionary ex-samurai called the League of the Divine Wind launched a surprise night-time attack on the castle in the city of Kumamoto on the southern island of Kyushu. As the barracks burned, they drove back the conscript soldiers of the Imperial Army, wounding hundreds and killing the wounded. Fires broke out everywhere. 'Even his garments, drenched in enemy blood, glowed crimson in the flames,' Mishima writes of one samurai. At last the soldiers regrouped and reached their guns and ammunition. The League, whose aim was to eradicate all traces of Westernisation and return Japan to its feudal past, had chosen to fight with swords. With no firearms, the samurai were decimated. The leader of the attack, gravely wounded, called on a follower to cut off his head. Most of the survivors committed seppuku.

Old buildings in Japan are seldom really old. A country that builds with wood instead of stone runs the constant risk of losing its monuments to fire. Ancient shrines are really copies of ancient shrines. The Imperial Palace in Kyoto has been rebuilt eight times, and its current layout would make no sense to any emperor who lived there. The main keep of Kumamoto Castle, which burned to the ground in another samurai uprising in 1877, was

SEICHŌ NO IE

Seichō no Ie is the most popular of Japan's 'new religions', with around 1.5 million followers (only a third of them in Japan). It was founded in 1930 by Taniguchi Masaharu, influenced by the American New Thought movement and Western culture more generally. It spread rapidly among the Japanese immigrant community in Brazil, which is home to most of its followers. Through meditation and gratitude to nature, family and ancestors, the movement's members affirm the creative power of thoughts and words; according to their doctrine, the material world, the human body and diseases do not exist, and all you need to do is tune in to a positive image of reality in order to influence it. This optimism combines well with a certain brand of turbo-charged capitalism (the Yaohan chain of shops used to distribute Seichō no Ie materials to its staff) as well as an uncommon degree of patriotism, which includes the adornment of altars with the Japanese flag, frequent references to the emperor and the conviction that the Japanese race plays a key role in history.

reconstructed from concrete in 1960. The forms return again and again. They end violently, and they never end at all. To live as a Japanese, Koga said, is to live the history of Japan.

His building is there. Koga's, I mean. In Kumamoto. Just down the hill from the castle. I found him a few hundred yards from the scene of the battle in the book that made me think of him in the first place.

The castle is on a hill in the centre of the city. There is a tiny car park at the base of the hill with a vending machine that sells Boss brand hot coffee. The castle's fortifications merge with the hillside just behind the car park, a tortoiseshell of large, dark stones too steep to climb.

His building is down the hill. A five-minute walk, if that. Come around the slope, and you will see the complex, a series of squat, identical grey blocks, each maybe eleven storeys tall. Cars speed by on a busy street. A security guard in a grey jacket and white motorcycle helmet stands beside the gate near some orange traffic cones. The complex's sign, printed in English on a black stone fence, is intersected at intervals by purple neon bars.

There is a bus stop very convenient for the building. There is a MaxValu just across the street.

*

So this is where I am. I am standing in the car park of the MaxValu. It is four o'clock in the afternoon. It is drizzly and cool. The cars that turn in to park are blunt, compact hatchbacks, little modern microvans in gold and pale blue and white. They are shaped like sumo wrestlers, I think, and it hits me that sumo is essentially a sport of refusing to die, refusing to be swept away, refusing to accept the insolidity of the dream. It was a street entertainment, really, until the early twentieth century.

Then the samurai tradition burned down and had to be rebuilt.

And soon I will think about this while I watch Hakuhō wrestle Kakuryū on the TV in my hotel room, on what is supposed to be the last match of the last day of the tournament: Hakuhō missing his chance to seize Kakuryū's *mawashi* just as Kakuryū wins a two-handed grip on his. Kakuryū literally leaping forward with spasmodic sliding jumps, backing the *yokozuna* to the edge of the rice-bale circle, where Hakuhō's knees and then his ankles will flex frantically, until he goes toppling, the greatest wrestler in the world, off the edge of the clay, twisting on to his stomach as he falls. When he gets to his feet Hakuhō will offer no reaction. A few minutes later, in the play-off match to break their identical 14-1 records, he will grapple Kakuryū in the middle of the ring and then drop his hips and lift Kakuryū halfway off the sand and force him backwards. They will both fall out of the ring at the same moment, but Kakuryū's foot will touch first, giving Hakuhō the Emperor's Cup and his twenty-eighth tournament championship. The *yobidashi* will sweep away the marks. Hakuhō will smile slightly, not a smile that is meant to be read.

But that will happen later. Now I am leaning on a railing in the car park of the MaxValu, thinking about endurance at four o'clock in the afternoon. I am looking across a busy street at the apartment complex of the man who beheaded Mishima Yukio and then lived a whole life afterwards, lived another forty years. I think: He is in there. I think: It is time to decide what to do.

I get up and move towards the pedestrian crossing. The wind is damp. It's January, so I don't see any butterflies. It is a cloudy day, so I do not see the moon.

Sweet Bitter Blues

Why are the Japanese so crazy about the blues? American journalist Amanda Petrusich ventures into the alleyways of Tokyo in search of an answer that seems to have more to do with the nature of Japanese culture than the exoticism of a distinctly African-American musical genre.

AMANDA PETRUSICH

Fabian Yūsuke, guitarist and singer in the Tokyo-based rock'n'roll and blues band the Minnesota Voodoo Men, in the sound-proofed one-room apartment where he lives and practises with his band.

The curling streets and alleyways of Shimokitazawa, a scrappy neighbourhood on the western edge of Tokyo, are too narrow to comfortably accommodate an actual automobile. But on foot a person can easily lose an afternoon wandering its attenuated paths, browsing racks of crumpled vintage T-shirts and shelves of enamel cookware, supping complicated, multi-ingredient cocktails. Tourist guides describe the area as 'endearingly haphazard' and 'meticulously inelegant'. It is, perhaps, a Japanese approximation of Brooklyn's approximation of some bohemian European enclave. Young people congregate in its bars and cafés, fiddling with devices, smoking, looking stylishly aggrieved.

I was in Shimokitazawa to see Steve Gardner, a singer and blues guitarist from Pocahontas, Mississippi, play a tiny club called Lown. American blues performers – purveyors of 'black music', as it is known colloquially here – can find good work in Tokyo and its immediate environs. I'd first gleaned something about the Japanese appreciation for specific tributaries of American vernacular music several years ago, when I was reporting a book about collectors of exceptionally rare 78 r.p.m. records. Artefacts of a certain era tended to drift peaceably but steadily across the Pacific – coaxed over, I was told, by affluent and eager bidders.

I couldn't quite figure out why Japanese listeners had come to appreciate and savour the blues in the way that they seemed to – lavishly, devotedly. Blues is still an outlier genre in Japan, but it's revered, topical, present. I'd spent my first couple of days in Tokyo hungrily trawling the city's many excellent record stores, marvelling at the stock. I had shuffled into the nine-storey Tower Records in Shibuya (NO MUSIC NO LIFE, a giant sign on its exterior read), past a K-pop band called CLC, an abbreviation for Crystal Clear – seven very young-looking women in matching outfits, limply performing a synchronised dance, waving their slender arms back and forth before a hypnotised crowd – and ridden an elevator to a floor housing more shrink-wrapped blues CDs than I have ever seen gathered in a single place of retail. I had been to a tiny, quiet bar – JBS, or Jazz, Blues and Soul – with floor-to-ceiling shelves housing owner Kobayashi Kazuhiro's eleven thousand LPs, from which he studiously selected each evening's soundtrack. I had seen more than one person wearing a Sonny Boy Williamson T-shirt. I had heard about

AMANDA PETRUSICH is a *New Yorker* journalist and music critic and the author of three books. Her articles have also appeared in *The New York Times*, *Pitchfork*, *GQ*, *Esquire*, *Playboy*, *The Nation* and *The Atlantic*. She was awarded the MacDowell Fellowship in 2015 and the Guggenheim Fellowship in non-fiction in 2016. In 2015 she was listed as one of the hundred most influential people in Brooklyn culture by *Brooklyn Magazine*. As well as music, her writing covers subcultures and travel.

audiophiles installing their own utility poles to get 'more electricity' straight from the grid to power elaborate sound systems. What I didn't know was what about this music made sense in Japan – how and why it had come to occupy the collective imagination, what it could offer.

*

A few hours before Gardner's set I ducked into a subterranean restaurant called the Village Vanguard; its name was presumably in homage to the famed New York City jazz club, although I could not discern any literal or even spiritual link between the two establishments. A sign on the door identified it as an 'almost hamburger shop'. I ordered the hamburger. Norman Rockwell prints were nailed to the walls alongside framed pages from *Life* magazine. 'Paradise City' bleated from overhead speakers. The decor evoked the interior of the roadhouse from *Thelma and Louise*, except the bar itself was tiki-themed, bedecked with lights and plastic tropical flowers. I was trying to develop some richer understanding of how the Japanese metabolise and reiterate notions of Americana, but the cumulative effect was dizzying – an incongruous amalgamation of signifiers. (I am certain that many Japanese-style restaurants in America feel just as insane to the Japanese.) I nibbled a French fry. There were licence plates from Illinois and Montana hanging above my table.

A jam session on the street outside the Big Mama, a vintage shop in Fussa, the dormitory town to the west of Tokyo that is home to the Yokota Air Base.

I'd made arrangements to meet up with the expat writer Michael Pronko, who was born in Kansas City but has lived in Tokyo for the past twenty years, teaching American literature, culture, film, music and art at Meiji Gakuin University. Pronko writes and edits for a website called Jazz in Japan, which features reviews, interviews and essays about Western music in Asia. I eventually found him waiting outside Shimokitazawa metro station wearing the hat, glasses and beard of a man who has travelled extensively – the grizzled-yet-refined comportment of a war correspondent. We repaired to a bar.

I figured Pronko might have ideas about why American blues resonates so strongly for some Japanese audiences. I already knew the rote socio-historical explanation – how African-American soldiers stationed in Japan during and after the Second World War had brought their record collections with them, and how an appreciation for those sounds (which were unfamiliar and, for many Japanese listeners, intoxicating) took root, flourished. This, of course, is also the story of every musical diaspora: a song or style travels, via commercially pressed records or sheet music or radio broadcasts or the performers themselves, and we are reminded anew that art transcends geography and that some expressions are so universally human as to be undeniable.

I was curious, though, about how this particular transmigration might be more complicated; blues, after all, is especially indebted to its place of provenance, the Deep South – specifically northwestern Mississippi and parts of Arkansas, Louisiana and Texas. To my ears, it is the most essentially American of all the great American idioms and contains a more literal retelling of its originating landscape than any other genre I can think of – there is a saturation and a heaviness to early blues, a doused

> "'When I play blues to students, I tell them not to listen to the words but to listen to the *feeling* of it – to the gut-punch. I think that kind of direct, emotional, uninhibited expression is really appealing to the Japanese, because things are so restrained in Japanese society.'"

but crackling heat, a flatness. This is one reason blues tourism continues to flourish in the Mississippi Delta. Fans share a pervasive belief that this music is perhaps best deciphered by more closely examining its wellspring, by coming to know the earth there, by steering the family sedan to the so-called Devil's Crossroads in Clarksdale, where Highways 61 and 49 intersect, and where, in the most apocryphal of all the great and concupiscent blues myths, Robert Johnson sold his soul to Satan so he could finger some hotter licks. Dazed-looking blues fans pull over, climb out of their cars, draw a lungful of soggy Southern air and, maybe, unlock some part of themselves. I've done it, is all I'm saying – I've gone there looking for answers. I found some.

Pronko and I ordered a round of beers. My theories were rickety, but I charged ahead nonetheless. I asked him about what I understood as a compelling tension between Japanese humility – a pervasive, unwavering stoicism – and the more unfettered spirit of the blues. These were grand, maybe irresponsible generalisations, but, even despite my broad strokes, a disconnection felt palpable. 'Blues is raw. There's no filter – [blues musicians] are often saying that they're angry, they're depressed,' Pronko agreed. 'In Japanese culture you tend to *not* express those things. To say "Oh, I feel terrible" is a burden on the other person, because then they're obligated to listen to you and take care of you. It's the same in America, maybe, but that obligation is stronger here,' he continued. 'When I play blues to students, I tell them not to listen to the words but to listen to the *feeling* of it – to the gut-punch. Do that first, then we'll get into the words. I think that kind of direct, emotional, uninhibited expression is really appealing to the Japanese, because things are so restrained in Japanese society.'

We finished our beers and eventually made our way to Lown, climbing a couple of flights of stairs (Tokyo, unlike most American cities, uses its vertical space in multi-purpose ways; storefronts aren't only at street level) into what appeared to be a small living room with a well-stocked bar. 'This is what's called a "live house",' Pronko said. 'Musicians rent it or make a deal with the owners to play here.' He'd mentioned earlier that he was often the only non-Japanese person in the audience at a blues show; watching the crowd gather, I understood what he meant. Pronko introduced me to Samm Bennett, another expat – Bennett was born and raised in Birmingham, Alabama – now working in Tokyo as a musician. We took seats along the back wall, in part because we were some of the tallest people in the room.

Steve Gardner was scheduled to play second. He was preceded by a folk duo called Magic Marmalade, who sang a beguiling acoustic song about a cactus named Linda

(according to my notes, it included the lyric 'Let us merge in the cosmic dance'). After their set, Gardner – a kind and jocular man, wearing jeans, suspenders and a white pork pie hat – made his way through the crowd and towards the stage carrying a National steel guitar. His voice is bulbous, rough, loud – equal parts Sam Elliott and Charley Patton. He pulled out a glass slide and opened with a rollicking version of 'Shady Grove', a traditional Appalachian folk song.

Gardner is a natural raconteur, and the crowd absorbed his banter readily. 'There really wasn't any blues until they figured out a way to sell it. Before it was recorded it was just music, and that's really how it oughta be, you know?' Gardner paused, worked out a few licks. 'Lots of great music was recorded by folks who couldn't see too well. A man named Blind Blake made this song, and I really do like it,' he offered. 'It's an old-time tune called "Police Dog Blues".'

'Police Dog Blues' was recorded in Richmond, Indiana, on 17 August 1929, for Paramount Records, a chair-company--turned-record-label based in Grafton, Wisconsin. Not a whole lot is known about Blake's life: he was born blind in 1896 in Newport News, Virginia, but also lived in Jacksonville, Florida, and parts of Georgia (it has been suggested that he sometimes spoke in a Geechee dialect – the creole language of the African-American Gullah people of some coastal areas of Georgia and South Carolina – indicating that he may have spent time in the Georgia Sea Islands). He began recording for Paramount in 1926 and made around eighty 78 r.p.m. sides for the company; for a pre-war country-blues

Guitarist Fabian Yūsuke plays in a jam session outside the Big Mama in Fussa.

Sweet Bitter Blues

performer he was remarkably prolific, which means he was also commercially successful. 'Police Dog Blues' is a song at least nominally about knowing when to give up on love. 'All my life I've been a travelling man,' Blake sings in his sweet, lapping voice, fingerpicking his guitar. 'I ship my trunk down to Tennessee, hard to tell about a man like me.'

Gardner's take was bigger, more out there. 'I met a gal, I couldn't get her off my mind,' he hollered; there was real desperation in his voice. Hearing it played this way, on the outskirts of Tokyo, sipping a sweating glass of Kentucky bourbon in a room full of rapt Japanese blues fans, it was spiritually rattling. According to my papers, I took only one tired, inscrutable note: 'This shit, same old shit, always the same.' The way things move. What makes us human.

*

When you are an American plotting your first trip to Tokyo and canvassing your network for tips, you will be told that the city is inscrutable to outsiders, and especially to Westerners. You will wonder if your colleagues are being hysterical when they say things like 'The streets don't have names' or 'There's a beautiful club, but I couldn't possibly tell you how to find it.'

It turns out that the Japanese addressing system is famously idiosyncratic. Tokyo is chock-a-block with tendrillar, lantern-lit alleyways that seem to circle in perpetuity – thousands of spiralling paths to God knows where. Street addresses, on the occasion that they are transcribed in Latin characters, tend to resemble lock combinations, like 2-10-305; this is technically the district, followed by the city block, followed by the house number, followed by a fourth number if your destination is an apartment. In Tokyo's more obscure pockets the buildings are not numbered consecutively (so ten might very well precede six). Even locals reference landmarks exclusively when attempting to offer a forgeable path. Like, 'Exit Shibuya station, take a left when you see three *izakaya* (traditional bars) in a row, take four more rights, take two quick lefts, walk up a steep hill, turn around, find the alleyway, look for a building with a snake in a terrarium in the window, then go to the third floor and knock a couple times – knock pretty hard.'

If you start searching the internet for help, thinking you are a real crackerjack reporter, you will end up on pages with titles such as 'The Black Art of Finding a Japanese Address' or – and this is in *The New York Times* – 'Tokyo, Where Streets Are Noodles'. That piece includes a telling exchange in which the writer implores a shopowner to divulge some tips. Was there some furtive trick non-locals could use to navigate the city? 'No,' said the owner, who declined to give his name. 'You have to just walk around, and that's the best way.'

I spent much of my time in Tokyo – eight days in late July – feeling glad but disquieted, perplexed. I am loath to recount any of this, because, of course, this is precisely how the narrative is always written: an American is set loose in Japan, and she is immediately adrift, rattled, roaming the streets in a kind of bewildered, lonesome daze. The bellwether of this particular canon (and it is staggeringly populous) is Sofia Coppola's 2003 film *Lost in Translation*, which recounts the odd, poignant relationship between Charlotte, a recent college graduate, and Bob, a waning film actor, as they wander Tokyo's opulent and hermetic Park Hyatt hotel, only periodically venturing beyond it. They are both searching intensely for something they can't, or don't feel ready to, name.

Charlotte (played by Scarlett Johansson)

is in Japan with her husband, a celebrity photographer on assignment; Bob (played by Bill Murray) is filming a series of commercials for Suntory whisky ('For relaxing times ... make it Suntory time!'). It's a beautiful and poetic film about yearning – or at least about reckoning with your own emptiness. It is also a movie about being tired, both literally – there's at least a thirteen-hour time difference between the east coast of the United States and Japan, meaning the day is rendered fully upside down, a flipped hourglass – and in more metaphysical ways.

The writer Joe Wood, in the opening paragraphs of his 1997 essay 'The Yellow Negro' in *Transition* magazine, about Japan's relationship to black culture, describes 'a sense of isolation' fastening to his brain 'like a lump of ice' upon his arrival in Tokyo from New York. I could see how Japan might be a place Americans travel to not merely to put distance between themselves and their regular lives but to render those lives incomprehensible; how, if your very existence has started to feel foreign to you, a satisfying solution might be to go to a place where your life is actually unrecognisable, to make real what you already know in your bones. This could account for the feelings of dissociation and loneliness that so often haunt these stories.

But surely there's also something about Tokyo's sheer size – 13.5 million people living within the city limits, and 38.5 million within the region, making it the world's most populous metropolitan area – that inevitably reminds a person her life is merely one of many lives, a realisation that sounds banal, even stupid, but can still trigger a funny kind of existential spiral. Then there's Japan's particular insularity: it's an island nation, culturally homogenous (recent figures suggest that around 98 per cent of the population identify as

MAKE IT SUNTORY TIME

The film *Lost in Translation* was released in 2003, and the year that Western cinemagoers saw Bill Murray advertising Suntory whisky was the same year that the Japanese spirit achieved proper recognition. Not so much thanks to Murray, obviously, as to the gold medal won by Yamazaki twelve-year-old (in fact, a product of the Suntory corporation) at the International Spirits Challenge. After that it was one triumph after another, and then, in 2014, the 2013 Yamazaki Sherry Cask beat all the Scottish single malts to become the world's best whisky, according to *Jim Murray's Whisky Bible*, the annual connoisseurs' guide. The main Japanese whisky producers are Suntory and Nikka, founded respectively by the pharmacist Torii Shinjirō in 1924 (the first distillery was in Yamazaki, between Osaka and Kyoto, in an area known for the exceptional quality of its water, where the legendary tea master Sen no Rikyū had built his own tea house) and his partner Taketsuru Masataka, who branched out on his own ten years later. Along with the purity of the waters, other factors in the quality of the whisky are the clear alternation of the four seasons, providing excellent ageing conditions, attention to detail and continuing adherence to artisan production methods – which are as faithful as possible to Scottish guidelines. The downside to this is that the distilleries are unable to keep pace with demand, leading to surging prices for certain bottles and the decision taken by some producers to abandon the ageing process.

> 'Masks, whether actual or metaphoric, are omnipresent here. "You can see a Japanese person visibly relax when they step into a club," Pronko continued. "It's a sacred space in that way."'

Japanese) and often wary of outsiders, or *gaijin*. Wandering Tokyo, I found it nearly impossible not to be continually reminded that I was a foreigner.

Ergo, that tourist's glaze: you are exhausted and instantly recognisable as an interloper, and counting buildings, and walking great and hilarious lengths in the exact wrong direction, and acclimatising poorly to the humidity, and bewildered by the language, and feeling sensitive about your life relative to every other life, and, somehow, in that confusion, a kind of cognitive dissociation occurs. A fissure. What emerges from that space is different for everyone. The film critic Elvis Mitchell wrote that *Lost in Translation* suggests 'a moment of evanescence that fades before the participants' eyes'. Many Western recollections of Tokyo share a similar vestigial quality: it is incomprehensible, liminal, hazy. And then it is gone.

*

Later that night, after his set, Gardner walked me towards the metro station and repeated the best way back to my accommodation. I suspect he saw on my face that I was the type of exhausted in which new information doesn't register quickly or well. After he turned to go back to the club, I encountered an ordinary-looking Japanese man in a dark-grey T-shirt, maybe nineteen or twenty years old, with his back to the street. There wasn't anyone else around; he was standing behind a leafy bush, near a closed grocery store. He'd huddled against the side of the building. An acoustic guitar hung from his neck by a length of rope. He was hunched over it, bent a little in the middle, playing a rollicking country-blues lick over and over and over again.

It was such a strange and private moment. I felt like I probably wasn't supposed to be there; I still don't know if he knew that I was. His playing was beautiful: sloppy and hot. Gleaming commuter trains passed overhead, reflecting in the storefront window, rumbling up to speed. I held my breath and took a nine-second video with my phone. This is the only reason I am certain that this happened.

*

A couple of weeks after I returned to the USA, Pronko shared some of his students' writings on the blues singer Bessie Smith with hopes that their pieces might further resolve some of my questions. Although his students were still learning English, I found their written reactions moving, trenchant. One, responding to Smith's fleshy 'Do Your Duty' from her final recording session in New York in 1933, admitted, 'In this song, she says "Do! Do! Do!" to her man. If I were her, I cannot say because of shameful things. But she say all things what she wants directly to her man with no shame so she is very cool. And these songs of Bessie Smith tell me or us it is OK to be so selfish so I was given courage after listening and studying these songs.'

Before arriving in Tokyo I'd read about

the Japanese phenomenon of *karōshi*, or death by overworking (see page 140). In 2008 *The Washington Post* reported on Japan's so-called 'killer work ethic', explaining that 'overtime rules remain so nebulous and so weakly enforced that the United Nations' International Labour Organization has described Japan as a country with no legal limits on the practice'. It's not especially unusual for a salaryman – as white-collar corporate workers are known here – to very suddenly collapse and die, usually after suffering some type of cardiac event or via a self-inflicted wound. Suicide is presently the leading cause of death for men aged twenty to forty-four in Japan, and it is not thought of as a particularly dishonourable or shameful way to die. (Kamikaze pilots, who led suicide attacks on Allied naval vessels, are still understood as heroic figures; this might be in part because the country has little history of Christianity, which declares suicide a sin.)

Pronko said he'd noticed the way Japanese salarymen seem to transform when they listen to music. 'Get me out of my thoughts, my obsession with work, and move me into some human experience,' he said. 'Let me stop thinking about this bullshit and start being a person.'

The idea of a deliberately concealed or shifting identity is essential to Japanese cultural history: Noh, which peaked some time in the mid-1300s, and kabuki, which began in the early 1600s, are two theatrical traditions that hinge upon the transformative and sometimes bewildering power of a literal mask (or, at least, very heavy makeup). Masks, whether actual or metaphoric, are omnipresent here. 'You can see a Japanese person visibly relax when they step into a club,' Pronko continued. 'It's a sacred space in that way. In the States you also go to hear music to stop your brain, to be different for a while. But it's less explicit because the pressure is less – you can be a human being at work in America. You can't always in Japan. You're at work, and whoever you are is kept inside so you can work. In the States you are who you are. You're a nice person, you're an asshole – you're the same at work.'

Was there something inherent in blues music that might facilitate this kind of loosening? It's a reductive distillation, but if you consider the challenge of Japanese work culture alongside the challenge of being a blues singer in the first few decades of the twentieth century (affluence versus impoverishment, marginalisation), the conditions can seem at odds, incompatible.

Still, I suspect that unhappiness itself – however it is borne – becomes a kind of password. It transcends its origins. The blues isn't always sorrowful, but it is usually wanting.

It seems possible to argue that American blues offers a new solution to the Japanese, an idea they maybe hadn't encountered before, hadn't realised could work as a balm. It's not merely a reflection of ennui or despair or confusion, it's a deep validation of it. It externalises the internal in a way that allows for catharsis.

But it's not a universal panacea. Pronko said that sometimes, in his experience, blues music is just too inexplicable for a Japanese listener to really connect to. 'It's a non-formalised experience,' he said. Such things are rare in Japan. 'You don't know what's gonna happen; you don't always know how the song is gonna turn out.' Pronko told me that improvisation as a concept is novel to his students. (I resisted a joke about my own university students, so beautifully capable of spontaneously inventing whole operatic responses to books they have not read.) 'It just doesn't translate. I have to explain it. Just the idea of not following the notes, not even looking

Above: The monthly jam session at Club Cactus in Tokyo; bluesman Iida Texas (top) and Texas with Nakamoto Taiki (bottom).
Pages 134–5: Nakamoto Taiki (left) and Fabian Yūsuke (right).

at the notes, not even having notes to look at – it blows their minds. *What do you mean, he's just playing it?*

*

I'd been told a good place to see Japanese musicians playing blues was a club called Blue Heat, in the Yotsuya neighbourhood of central Tokyo. When I pulled up in a taxi, around 9 p.m., I saw its big, glowing sign first: LIVE AND BLACK MUSIC BAR BLUE HEAT. When I went inside the building there was a canary-yellow sticker reading 'Real Black Music!!' affixed to its mailbox.

Judging by the signs dividing up the record bins in Tokyo, 'black music' is a genre unto itself in Japan, and it encompasses hip-hop, R&B, gospel, soul, funk, blues and jazz. (This bracketing phenomenon called to mind, for me, the scene in *This Is Spinal Tap* – the spoof 'rockumentary' directed by Rob Reiner in 1984 satirising the world of heavy rock – in which David and Nigel, recounting the spontaneous combustion of their drummer, bicker lightly about whether the festival they were playing was a 'jazz-blues festival' or a 'blues-jazz festival, really'.) That these are very distinct traditions in America seemed somewhat irrelevant here, perhaps in part because Japan has so few black citizens.

The national census doesn't enquire about race or ethnicity, merely nationality, so it remains difficult to find precise numbers about the country's racial makeup. (In my brief time exploring Tokyo I somehow saw just one black person, the recording artist Ben Harper, strolling through a park with a companion.) In 2015 a half-Japanese, half-American couple – Rachel and Jun Yoshizuki – made a YouTube documentary, *Black in Japan*, exploring the experience via interviews with seven African Americans and one Jamaican living in the country. Their subjects' impressions are largely positive, although they do recount being photographed without permission, having their hair touched by strangers and being called 'Whitney Houston'. Most said they still felt safer in Japan than in America.

Joe Wood, wandering the streets near Tokyo's Shinjuku station, met a more unwelcome gaze. 'I thought I could detect an ugly fascination in the eyes of the people around me,' he writes in 'The Yellow Negro'. 'How bizarre that there should be such malevolence toward blacks in a country with almost no black people.' Wood discusses his fear of encountering Sambo, the contentious title character from *The Story of Little Black Sambo*, a children's book written and illustrated by the Scottish author Helen Bannerman in 1899 featuring a young, dark-skinned boy with hugely exaggerated features; until recently Sambo iconography remained oddly popular in Japan. In 1932 Langston Hughes described the book as 'amusing undoubtedly to the white child, but like an unkind word to one who has known too many hurts to enjoy the additional pain of being laughed at'.

The problem with trying to mindfully unpack Japan's blues fandom is that even the most expansive theories require condensing whole cultures – to say nothing of individual tastes – into representative sums. Occasionally, those sums feel like dangerous projections. In his essay *The White Negro: Superficial Reflections on the Hipster* Norman Mailer argues that Beat writers were drawn to and impressed by jazz and blues because the players 'gave voice to the character and quality of [the musician's] existence, to his rage and the infinite variations of joy, lust, languor, growl, cramp, pinch, scream, and despair of his orgasm'. Through that, they could achieve a kind of proxy freedom, a rejection of what they understood whiteness to be: a buttoned-up, suburban lifestyle in which

KARŌSHI

Hundreds of people in Japan die each year through overwork – this sudden work-related demise is known as *karōshi* – usually by strokes or heart attacks brought on by exertion, stress and starvation diets or by committing suicide (*karōjisatsu*). These deaths are just the tip of the iceberg if you also take into account those caused only in part by problems in the workplace. The first case of *karōshi* was reported in 1969, and the Ministry of Labour has published statistics since 1987. (Japan is one of the few countries, along with China and South Korea and a few others, where the phenomenon is sufficiently widespread for there to be a need to keep count. Cases have also occurred in Europe, however, the most famous being that of Moritz Erhardt, an intern at Bank of America Merrill Lynch in London, who died in 2013 after working seventy-two hours straight.) Only in recent years has the government started taking measures, in the light of famous cases such as the death of TV journalist Sado Miwa from a heart attack at the age of thirty-one and the suicide of 24-year-old Takahashi Matsuri, who was working for the advertising giant Dentsu (a company that once wrote in its staff manual: 'Once you start, you do not give up – even if it kills you'). These measures are often merely symbolic, however, such as Premium Friday, when companies are encouraged to shut up shop at 3 p.m. on the last Friday of the month, and they do not tackle what experts regard as the fundamental problem, the overtime culture built on the twin values of loyalty (to the company) and honour, which is also seen as an obstacle to women's access to the workplace.

emotion was stifled or politely presented, rather than loosed and celebrated. This, obviously, is a preposterous and troubling fantasy, hinging on, among other things, the presumption that black Americans are free of inhibitions, unattached, hypersexual, primitive and inherently better at expressing bodily anguish or ecstasy.

The idea of being attracted to something by virtue of its exoticism has been nothing but trouble historically. (The Japanese themselves have been subject to this for centuries; the American social justice activist Andrea Smith once named orientalism one of the 'three pillars of white supremacy'.) But because Japanese culture is so insular, and because there are so few other races established here, it seems likely that Japanese music fans might have come to regard American blues musicians – most of whom were indigent and nearly all of whom were black – as curiosities.

Still, as far as I could tell – and, because of the language barrier, many of my conversations with actual Japanese blues fans were mimed interactions; this is not the most sophisticated way to communicate multiform ideas about anything, let alone the blues diaspora – the Japanese are interested in blues and jazz less for their strangeness and more for their complexity. For a non-native English speaker, blues, with its endless idioms and idiosyncrasies, requires work to understand. It demands studiousness.

'Japanese see blues as being this really difficult form to master,' Pronko told me. 'It's hard to play it well, and singing it is even more challenging. I think they respect it for the complex music that it is. The racial aspect is nearly secondary,' he said.

The blues, then, becomes a daunting intellectual challenge. 'A lot of bands here are called "copy bands" – they'll play the

The Tokyo-based rock'n'roll and blues band the Minnesota Voodoo Men in the sound-proofed one-room apartment where guitarist and singer Fabian Yūsuke (centre) lives and rehearses with the band: drummer Pete (left) and Ringo, bass and vocals (right).

Sweet Bitter Blues

Fabian Yūsuke of the Minnesota Voodoo Men.

Allman Brothers or Stevie Ray Vaughan or the Meters. These are bands that just work on capturing the sound of their particular band. From an American point of view, it seems false – "copy" sounds bad in America. But it doesn't have that feeling here,' he continued. 'To play a Stevie Ray Vaughan song well – that's not so easy! To play well in an imitative way, it isn't a shameful thing at all. There's no hesitation to *be like* somebody.' This helps explain, in part, why karaoke – a Japanese creation – remains so wildly popular in Japan. In the States, cover bands (and karaoke parlours) are certainly present, but that American drive for true, seismic innovation – that frontier spirit, that deep thirst for ownership, the desire to venture where no one has gone before and claim a plot in your name – is paramount.

At Blue Heat, both the crowd and the band were exclusively Japanese. The audience was younger than I'd been expecting: couples who appeared to be in their late twenties or early thirties, crowded around long tables, smiling, smoking, clinking bottles of beer. The men wore skinny ties, and the women were in fashionable dresses and boots. The band, a four-piece – two acoustic guitars, an electric bass and drums – was called Sweet Bitter Blues, which I only know from the half-English sign I saw posted by the entrance (the same sign also identified the guitarist and lead vocalist's name as Blues'n Curtain, although no other players were ID'd in English). The interior was painted a dull black, and fading posters taped on the walls commemorated blues events of yesteryear: Otis Rush in 1966; the James Cotton Band. There were many shelves of vinyl records.

I took a seat at the bar. After a little banter in Japanese and titters from the crowd, the band launched into Ray Charles's 'Hallelujah I Love Her So', a gospel hymn Charles adapted and released in 1956 (it was later covered by Jerry Lee Lewis, Harry Belafonte, Frank Sinatra and, most famously, the Beatles). Their set was composed mostly of covers. Hearing Allen Toussaint's 'Play Something Sweet (Brickyard Blues)', a hit for Three Dog Night in 1974, sung enthusiastically and in a very strong Japanese accent while an approving crowd claps along is, I can say now with certainty, a singular musical experience. Blues'n Curtain was wearing a vintage Louisville Cardinals T-shirt and a busker's cap. His performance was jubilant.

After the show I stopped for a nightcap in Tokyo's Golden Gai district, a corner of the Shinjuku neighbourhood known for its clustering of tiny bars – six narrow alleyways, some of which barely allow for a whole person to pass through, leading to more than two hundred ramshackle taverns, most containing fewer than a dozen seats. I wandered into a place called Slow Hand, in part because its sign read EVERY DAY I HAVE THE BLUES.

'Oh, buddy,' I murmured to no one in particular.

Inside, I surveyed the ephemera: posters for *The Blues Brothers*, Eric Clapton, the Butterfield Blues Band, Frank Zappa. A giant, curling portrait of Robert Johnson. I was the only patron. I ordered a Japanese whisky, which arrived in a heavy, cut-crystal glass. The bartender – and lone employee – set out an ashtray decorated with peace signs and the words HAIGHT-ASHBURY and began fixing me an octopus and miso salad, although I hadn't asked for anything to eat. We tried to chat, but mostly we mimed, laughed. He told me a confusing but nonetheless thrilling story about John Mayer and Katy Perry coming in and ordering a bunch of drinks. The punchline was either 'Suntory!' or 'Katy Perry!' I inexpertly poked at a chunk of octopus with a chopstick. He put on a DVD of *Blues Masters*, a CBC documentary about a three-day recording session held in Toronto in 1966 that included Muddy Waters, Willie Dixon and James Cotton. He said his favourite piano player was Sunnyland Slim, who was born in the Delta but moved to Chicago in 1942, part of the Great Migration of black southern workers to the industrialised north.

Eventually, he pulled out a ukulele from under the bar and played me a heartbreaking if imperfect version of 'What a Wonderful World'. I tried to pretend that some dust had got in my eyes.

*

I'd arranged to meet Samm Bennett in the late afternoon outside Shibuya station. We sat down at the only nearby bar that was open, a British-style pub, and ordered Bloody Marys. Michelle Branch's 'All You Wanted' was playing on the house stereo. Bennett was born in Alabama and weaned on the Allman Brothers, the Beatles. 'I grew up in a middle-class suburb. It's not like there were bluesmen on the corner,' he said, laughing.

In 1995 he moved to Tokyo from New York City, exclusively to play music – jazz, blues and his own experimental reworkings of both. 'I first came here to play concerts in 1986. There was a connection between the downtown New York scene and certain Japanese musicians, and I got invited over to do some shows. After that, I came to Japan about once a year, almost always with a saxophonist named Umezo Kazutoki. We were doing free improvisation – not an extremely austere thing, we did a lot of grooves. The term "jam band" didn't exist back then, but we were kind of a jam band.'

Bennett was understandably reluctant to make generalisations about why blues remains popular in Japan, but he did acknowledge a gulf. 'I think a lot actually gets lost in translation. Really liking something and really *understanding* it are two different things,' he said. 'People really love the blues here. That doesn't mean that they're catching all the inflections. When Japanese people play the blues themselves – and I hesitate to say this – there's something almost grafted on. It's not something that's entirely ...' He paused. 'The word "natural" is really loaded – everybody has to learn. But the really good players master certain styles instrumentally. Vocally, it's another thing. Blues, in particular, demands a certain kind of character. Even the best jazz singers aren't that great when they sing the blues. I think it's a question of feel.'

After Bennett split to prepare for *Drunk Poets See God*, the monthly English-language poetry and music show he hosts, I took the train to Nakano City, a ward west of Tokyo proper. I'd been told there was a blues club there called Bright Brown, a kind of epicentre of the scene. I wandered the neighbourhood for a while, eating conveyor-belt sushi, drinking cups of sake, popping into *izakaya*. I tried my luck at one of those bleeping, apocalyptically lit arcades full of claw machines, attempting to fish out (in order): a giant stuffed cat, a giant stuffed banana, a small stuffed doughnut and something that looked like an overfed gerbil. I left empty handed.

By the time I found Bright Brown – this involved walking past it approximately thirty-five times – a Chicago-style blues guitarist named Hurricane Yukawa had just taken the stage. I tried to linger inconspicuously in the back, but a barkeep emerged and kindly led me to an open seat at a table full of young Japanese, who immediately offered me the plates of tomato salad and cheese and crackers they'd been sharing. There were framed pictures of American bluesmen on the wall, and a small disco

KARAOKE: A PERSISTENT PASTIME

The phenomenon of getting together in groups to sing to music has perhaps always existed, but it was a Japanese musician by the name of Inoue Daisuke who invented the first karaoke machine in 1971 (the name derives from the combination of the Japanese words for empty, *kara*, and orchestra, *ōkesutora*), bringing the craze to restaurants and hotel rooms. Inoue Daisuke, who did not patent his invention, won the satirical IgNobel Peace Prize in 2004 for 'providing people with an entirely new way to learn to tolerate each other'. In Asian countries, karaoke usually takes place in karaoke boxes, private rooms hired by the hour, where you can order food and drink by computer (the phenomenon of *wankara*, or single-occupant boxes, is also becoming increasingly common). The Japanese make a clear distinction between Saturday karaoke with friends and after-work karaoke with colleagues and clients, in which etiquette demands, for instance, that you do not sing the boss's *ohako* (favourite song), that you avoid sad, risqué or obscure songs and that you practise singing at least three duets in case the boss requests them. Karaoke reached its peak in the mid-1990s when around half the population of Japan claimed to have taken part at least once. Innovations such as apps and karaoke taxis have taken customers away from traditional venues, which have also been hit by scandals linked to prostitution, as well as the reduction in free time and young people's purchasing power.

ball hung from the ceiling; the room was warm and crowded and lit by strings of white Christmas lights. I ordered a whisky.

Yukawa was playing with a pianist, a Japanese woman in a white T-shirt and black jeans who didn't seem much older than thirty. Her hands appeared to be moving fully independent of the rest of her body – this is the case with all the best blues pianists – her fingers levitating over the keys and then striking suddenly, fiercely, like a snake winding through tall grass. Yukawa was playing a Fender Telecaster and expertly running through the post-war Chicago blues songbook – 'Pitch a Boogie Woogie If It Takes Me All Night Long', the Howlin' Wolf catalogue. He had slicked-back hair and a generously unbuttoned shirt. Between songs Yukawa bantered amiably with the audience. The spirit was jovial, easy. During a break in the set I had what felt like a fairly sophisticated conversation about *Rolling Stone* magazine with a man wearing a loosened tie, although the only words either of us actually said were 'Rolling' and 'Stone'. At one point another of my tablemates, who had seen me scribbling in a notebook, pointed at me and yelled, 'American writer!'

Everyone laughed hysterically.

Sweet Bitter Blues

Family Album

Following the huge success of Kore-eda Hirokazu's *Shoplifters*, winner of the 2018 Palme d'Or at Cannes, we survey how families are portrayed in Japanese cinema. From young people struggling to break free of their parents in Ozu Yasujirō's post-war masterpieces through to the indifference of contemporary society and alternative families, we go on a journey that deconstructs the myth of the 'typical' Japanese family.

GIORGIO AMITRANO
Translated by Jennifer Higgins

The Kodaka family in their Tokyo apartment; on the left, Masumi with her son Kazusa, and on the right her husband Kazuki.

There is one theme that occurs more frequently than any other in contemporary Japanese films, no matter the genre: the family. In comedies and anime, yakuza tales and thrillers alike, the insidious tentacles of blood relationships snare people in their grasp. Even in *jidaigeki* period dramas and J-horror, the intrigues of love, loyalty and grudges generated by families are inexhaustible sources of inspiration.

In this ocean of cinematographic production, the oldest examples of which date back to the silent-film era, one particular work shines out like a beacon: Yasujirō Ozu's *Tokyo Story* (*Tōkyō monogatari*, 1953). This is regularly cited internationally as one of the greatest films of all time and also one of the most moving, authentic and universal representations of the family ever produced anywhere – all the more remarkable, given that Ozu's films became well known outside Japan much later than those of his contemporaries such as Kurosawa Akira and Mizoguchi Kenji, because Ozu's own producers thought his work too Japanese and therefore incomprehensible to foreigners. This restrictive view was certainly not shared by Ozu himself who, like many directors of his generation, was a connoisseur of non-Japanese cinema and had made it his own. Perhaps the producers were not even aware that *Tokyo Story* was inspired by an American film, Leo McCarey's *Make Way for Tomorrow* (1937); Ozu and his faithful filmmaking and drinking companion, screenwriter Noda Kōgo, took their inspiration from one of its main themes: young people's intolerance of their ageing, provincial parents. *Tokyo Story* follows an older couple visiting their children, who had left home for Tokyo many years before. The children receive them coldly, treating them as a burden from which they want to be free as soon as possible. Only the daughter-in-law, a widow whose husband died during the war, is genuinely pleased to see them and gives them a warm welcome. After the parents return home the mother dies, and the whole family is reunited for the funeral, but not even this is enough to overcome the children's indifference, and they are anxious to return to the city and take their places in the relentless machinery of urban life.

Like many masterpieces, *Tokyo Story* evokes the realities of its time perfectly. Poetic in its graceful depictions of human behaviour but precise in its sociological observation, the film transports us into the climate of the early 1950s when Japan, still engaged in reconstruction, was preparing the foundations for its future economic boom. Ozu's light touch and moderation suggest the idea of an essentially harmonious society in which conflicts tend to be resolved or, at worst, set aside without

GIORGIO AMITRANO is professor of Japanese language and literature at the University of Naples 'L'Orientale'. Formerly director of the Italian Cultural Institute in Tokyo, he is the translator of some of the most important voices in contemporary Japanese literature, from Murakami Haruki to Yoshimoto Banana and Kawabata Yasunari. His most recent book, *Iro Iro* (De Agostini, 2018), pays tribute to the country where he once lived and to which he has devoted his life.

trauma, small ripples in the tranquil flow of existence. Nevertheless, within the apparent serenity of his nuclear families Ozu hints that personal interest wins out over solidarity and that love is difficult to separate from emotional blackmail. The subtext of many of his films is that belonging to the family microcosm inevitably entails giving up a part of oneself. There is, then, an element of bitter disenchantment that makes Ozu's work more problematic than is generally recognised.

Many decades after Ozu, another filmmaker producing masterful depictions of families is the contemporary director Kore-eda Hirokazu. Highly esteemed in the West – he has won several prizes at international festivals, including the 2018 Palme d'Or at Cannes for *Shoplifters* (*Manbiki kazoku*, 2018) – Kore-eda is widely seen as Ozu's heir, a label that doesn't appear to sit comfortably with him. However, his focus on family themes, the wisdom with which he directs his actors, his ability to use the urban landscape as a counterpoint to human affairs and, above all, his acute sensitivity to the inner workings of families concealed in the fabric of daily life all point to an undeniable affinity with the old master. But the similarities end there. For example, Kore-eda, despite the pastel tones of some of his family portraits, doesn't hesitate to tackle stories with high dramatic potential, as he did in *Nobody Knows* (*Dare mo shiranai*, 2004) and in *Shoplifters*. Both films are based on actual events, extreme episodes that don't reflect the reality of the typical Japanese family but express anxiety and imbalance that are more common than we might think. *Nobody Knows*, as the title suggests, is a critique of a society indifferent and impassive in the face of suffering, a society that doesn't know, and doesn't want to know, about anything that doesn't concern it directly. A single mother with four children by different partners rents a flat in a large apartment block. She doesn't tell the landlords about the three younger children in case they get thrown out. The children are thus forced to hide and forbidden to go out. Having been used to this clandestine life from birth, they find it natural and don't question it or try to rebel. In any case, they would be unable to engage with other people, having never been to school or spent any time with other children. In the meantime, the mother goes to live elsewhere, returning every so often to bring them money, but her visits eventually cease, and the children are left to look after themselves. The eldest, a boy of around twelve, takes charge, but despite his sense of responsibility he can't prevent himself and his brothers gradually falling into a state of neglect. Hungry and tired, with neither water nor electricity, both having been cut off because the bills haven't been paid, the children break the rule about never showing themselves. They leave the house and begin to roam the neighbourhood, but even then they remain invisible to a society that continues to ignore them until the accidental death of one of them transforms the drama into a tragedy.

Nobody Knows is a painful, understated

A vintage studio portrait of Masumi and Kazuki in wedding outfits.

reflection of the level of alienation in Japanese society during the boom years. The events on which the film is loosely based occurred in 1988, a key moment in the *baburu*, the bubble economy, which, having created immense wealth, burst in 1992, dragging Japan into an unprecedented economic crisis. The mother in *Nobody Knows* is poles apart from a great many other characters in Japanese cinema, especially those in older works, whose sense of duty towards their family borders on total self-sacrifice. This comparison with the noble figures of the past could lead some to the rash conclusion that Japanese society has, over the course of the last fifty years, lost all humanity and that the institution of the family has today fallen into irreparable decadence. But between the two poles – a self-punishing notion of duty in the past and a form of pathological egotism in the present – there is a wide range of other voices: stories of families in which a sense of responsibility is not a divine imperative but a hard-won achievement and where it is possible to negotiate the edge of the precipice without necessarily falling into it with disastrous results.

The Sound of the Mountain (*Yama no oto*, 1954) is an example of this more problematic and nuanced approach. It is the work of the director Naruse Mikio, less well known than the great triumvirate of Kurosawa, Ozu and Mizoguchi but their artistic equal. The film is an adaptation of the novel of the same name by Kawabata Yasunari, and it succeeds in recreating the essence of the book's characters and atmosphere with great skill. The result is all the more extraordinary given that the novel is a kind of interior third-person monologue, in which events become mixed up with the perceptions of the protagonist, a sixty-year-old man named Shingo. Kawabata was long considered an aesthete, cloistered in an elegant, rarefied world, but *The Sound of the Mountain* shows his profound understanding of the social mechanisms of his time and how they interact with family dynamics. The country that he depicts is more or less the Japan we see in *Tokyo Story*: a country shattered by war but already on the path to economic rebirth. In this film, too, we find two ageing parents: Shingo and Yasuko. Shūichi, their eldest son, lives with them with his wife Kikuko. The younger daughter, Fusako, has run away from her husband and comes to take refuge with her parents, bringing her daughters with her. Shingo's relationship with his wife is held in place by ties of long habit and respect, but he has never felt admiration or desire for her. Shūichi's relationship with his wife is in crisis: his experiences during the war have made him cynical and cold, and he has a lover, meaning that he devotes very little time and attention to Kikuko. Fusako is jealous of her sister-in-law and hostile towards her parents, who she feels do not offer her enough love or protection. In the midst of this web of difficult and sometimes hostile family relationships, Shingo and Kikuko begin to develop an affectionate friendship that comes close to love without ever crossing the line. Their emotional exchange is one of silent empathy. Nothing as corrosive as complicity ever grows between them, only silent interpretation of each other's movements and a desire to observe what the other has observed – a gingko sapling emerging, the defiant beauty of a sunflower – so that thoughts not bodies touch one another and become intertwined.

The film creates a delicate balance between subtle representations of the characters' states of mind, which the director expresses through discreet and suggestive framing and lucidly realistic depictions of the era. This allows the film, like the novel, to communicate the huge transformation that Japan was undergoing during the late 1940s and early 1950s. During the Allied occupation a law had been passed establishing the husband and wife as the fundamental unit of the family, abolishing the traditional role of the parent–child relationship as the main axis of domestic life. This transition from the patriarchal family to the nuclear family is reflected in the film when a final choice is made by Shingo, who announces to his daughter-in-law that she and her husband must go and live together elsewhere. It is an intense moment: for Shingo and Kikuko it means the end of the shared thoughts and observations that had satisfied them both, but, although they don't know it, this separation also represents their adaptation to changing times.

Just as memorable, although from a different era and in a different style, is Morita Yoshimitsu's *The Family Game* (*Kazoku gēmu*, 1983). The director depicts a typical middle-class family, the Numatas, at a time when Japan was one of the richest and most productive countries in the world and where consumerism and competition ruled. The father is a salaryman, a white-collar office worker (see page 174), and the mother a housewife. They have two sons, one in middle school, the other in high school. The younger boy, Shigeyuki, isn't doing well in his studies, and, as the dreaded high-school entrance exam approaches, the parents employ a young man to coach him. This tutor introduces subversive elements into the peaceful routine of this 'normal family'. The caresses and compliments that he gives to the boy – at one point he even kisses him – initially seem like the beginnings of *sekuhara* (sexual abuse), but it is a seduction technique that also takes in other family members, including the father, with the goal of being welcomed unreservedly into the family. Once the tutor has gained Shigeyuki's trust, he next begins to assert his power over him by beating him up. The boy is in shock, but the man's behaviour, for all its violence, exerts an authority over him that his father has never even tried to wield. The teacher doesn't stop at beating the boy; he teaches him to fight and defend himself, helping him to rebel against the bullying he suffers at school. The film constantly wrong-foots the viewer, who can never understand fully what is happening. The tutor's appearance at the beginning of the movie resembles that of the mysterious, seductive guest who visits the bourgeois family in Pier Paolo Pasolini's *Teorema*, and, as the film progresses, his ambiguous role is reminiscent of Joseph Losey's *The Servant*. When he teaches the boy to defend himself we are suddenly closer to the realm of Victor Fleming's *Captains Courageous*. The biggest surprise comes in the final scene, when the family get together for a dinner to celebrate Shigeyuki's exam success. The tutor begins to spread food all over the table, throwing noodles everywhere, spilling wine and physically assaulting his fellow diners. This surreal, transgressive scene takes us in a completely new direction, somewhere between Buñuel and

Photograph from the Tsuchiya family album showing Keiko's father and Kotoko's ex-husband.

The Tsushiya family at their home in Shiroi, Chiba Prefecture; on the left is Keiko, wife of Osami (right) and daughter of Kotoko (centre, holding Alice the robot dog).

The Kobayashi sisters with their mother in the family home in Hiratsuka, Kanagawa Prefecture, where all three have lived since the mother fell ill; Mana is on the left, Kinuko is in the centre and Chinatsu is on the right.

Family Album

Masumi and cat in the Tokyo apartment where she lives with her husband and son.

the Dušan Makavejev of *Sweet Movie*. The viewer eventually stops seeking comparisons and, once the initial disorientation passes, enters into the world created by Morita. The Numata family is a metaphor for Japan, a country chasing after illusory success that has lost touch not only with the supposed values of self and identity linked to the traditional past but also with reality. The Numatas have become wealthy, and this has led them to live in a huge apartment building, a ghostly non-place built on an artificial island in Tokyo Bay. They are completely focused on such objectives as getting their sons into exclusive schools, the first step towards places at prestigious universities, which, in turn, guarantee brilliant careers. Relationships within the family are vacuous, impersonal and 'scripted'. With his aggressive behaviour the tutor introduces a hefty dose of reality, which the family choose to accept only for its 'useful' purpose (of improving the son's academic results) and not when it questions the mediocrity of their lives. This is a black comedy, both provocative and extremely funny.

So much for 'normal' families. What about alternative families? There are many representations of these, which might come as a surprise to those familiar only with the image of Japan as a rule-based society that upholds respect for the older generation.

Kore-eda depicts a far from ordinary family in *Shoplifters*, one that is damaged but nonetheless rich in humanity in a society that runs efficiently but lacks sensitivity.

Photograph from the Kobayashi family album.

This is a dysfunctional microcosm whose members look after one another and show high levels of physical affection. As the film progresses we learn that this is not actually a family in the strictest sense of the word – there is no blood tie linking its members, whom circumstance has brought together. The two children have been 'kidnapped'; the quotes here show my hesitation to use a term that doesn't do justice to the new parents' desire to save the children from lives of neglect and, in at least one case, abuse. These 'acquired' children are taught how to shoplift, and they become skilled in distracting shop assistants while they steal food and goods. The common perception of Japan as a country where petty crime is almost non-existent is turned on its head by this film, in which theft is carried out nonchalantly and taught to children. But the viewer is obliged to call something far deeper into question: the idea that a certain level of inhumanity is an acceptable price to pay for living in a safe, efficient society. Kore-eda casts doubt on values that seemed to be taken as given.

Another film to feature alternative families is *Hush!* (*Hasshu!*, 2001), Hashiguchi Ryōsuke's story of Asako, a young woman who wants to involve a gay male couple in her plan to become a mother. When the men's families learn about their sons' homosexuality and Asako's request they intervene and, during a tense, uncomfortable meeting, condemn Asako's behaviour. She defends herself, saying, 'I just wanted to choose my own family.' The mother of one of the men replies, 'Family isn't something you choose!' This exchange encapsulates the collision between irreconcilable visions of the family. It's an issue that Japan is only just beginning to confront, and this film is ahead of its time in focusing on it. Japanese society is libertarian when it comes to sexual behaviour but rigid in opposing changes that threaten its traditional structure.

Cinema has a wider vision, though, and films in which the depiction of the family is one of a restless, constantly changing organism are far more numerous than films showing a respectful, sugar-coated image of socially acceptable structures. Even in genre films there are examples of families that don't exactly correspond to traditional norms. One of the most successful *chanbara*, or samurai, films (a popular subset within the *jidaigeki* genre) was the *Lone Wolf and Cub* (*Kozure ōkami*) cycle, a series of six films made between 1972 and 1974 following the fortunes of a samurai fighting against a fierce clan who want to kill him. The protagonist, Ogami Ittō, is left alone with his small baby after his wife dies at the beginning of the first film. He has been working as an executioner for the shogun but is forced to flee after the Yagyū clan plot to kill him. He takes his baby, Daigorō, with him. An unrivalled swordsman, Ogami defeats innumerable enemies over the course of the six films, always with his child beside him in a wooden pram. Ogami's paternal love is movingly depicted. At the beginning of the first film he is prepared to kill his son: he offers the little boy a choice between a tempting coloured ball and a sword, and if the boy had chosen the sword Ogami would have killed him. Once this test is passed, the father protects his son in every way he can from the dangers that constantly lie in wait for them. And there are many dangers: their path is one of severed limbs, dismembered corpses, raped and murdered women and endless spurts of blood lavish enough to send Quentin Tarantino into ecstasies. (Tarantino is, unsurprisingly, an admirer of the series, and *Kill Bill* is partly inspired by it.) During one attack the young Daigorō uses a mechanism hidden inside his pram to release a spear that pierces the enemy's heart. The fellowship between this indomitable warrior and his baby is perhaps not the most typical example of a traditional family, but the success of this series, which is based on a hugely popular manga by Koike Kazuo and Kojima Gōseki, shows that family ties can appear and grow even in the most unexpected environments and can elicit tears and sincere emotion from viewers. The duo of Ittō and Daigorō demonstrates a mutual solidarity and a shared purpose rarely seen in a 'real' family.

All this raises the question of whether the family as portrayed in film – be it anarchic or respectful of the rules, orthodox or alternative, patriarchal or nuclear – might have a stronger, more easily distinguishable physiognomy than that of many less clearly defined families that we encounter in real life, families that seem caught in a crisis the origins of which are now forgotten and whose end is not within sight. It is a crisis of parental authority, of adolescents increasingly closed in on themselves, ever lower birth rates, increasing longevity ... These are problems that families prefer not to confront, instead hiding behind a façade of respectability and enjoying the benefits of their material wealth. One thing is certain, and I hope that this brief reflection has illustrated it: Japanese cinema paints a picture of the family and of society that is far less respectable, far more diverse and contradictory and ultimately far richer than families and society would like to admit.

POPULATION OF JAPAN

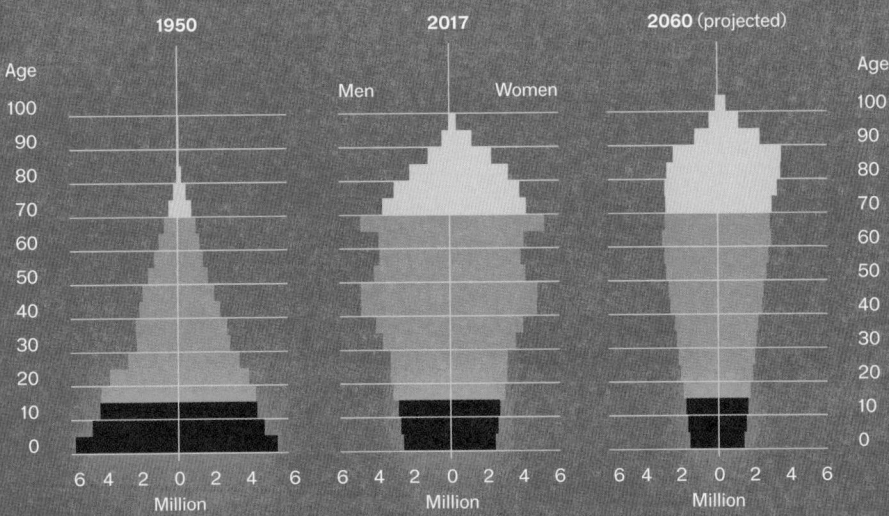

PERCENTAGE OF CHILDREN BORN OUTSIDE MARRIAGE

///// 1980   ■ 2007

- Iceland: 40 / 66
- UK: 12 / 44
- USA: 18 / 40
- **Japan**: 1 / 2

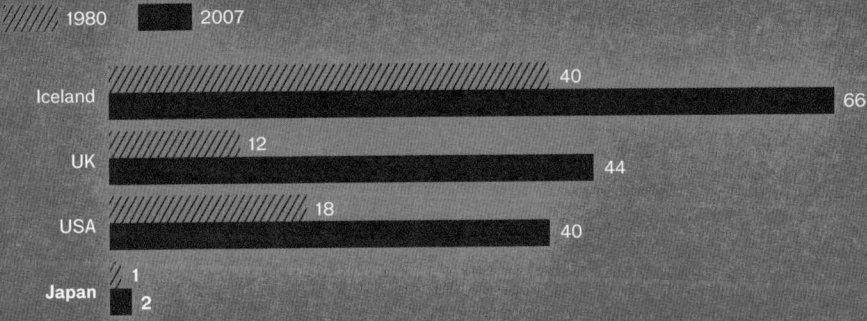

CENTENARIANS PER 100,000

- **Japan**: 48
- Portugal: 38.9
- USA: 22
- UK: 21.5
- Russia: 4.8
- China: 3.6
- India: 2.1

Estimated global figure: 6.2

SOURCE: WIKIPEDIA. POPULATION STATISTICS OF JAPAN

PERCENTAGE OF THE POPULATION UNMARRIED AT 50

—— Women   ······ Men

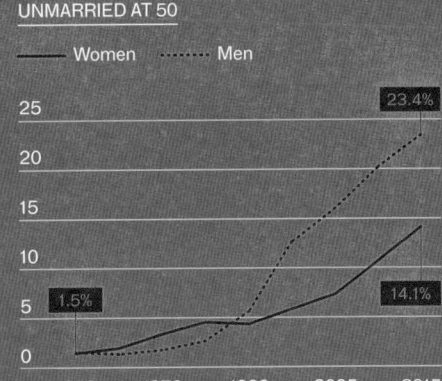

1.5% — 23.4% — 14.1%

Family Album

The Evaporated

After abruptly disappearing to make a new life elsewhere, tens of thousands of Japanese are living in the shadows to escape debt. This astonishing phenomenon derives from a tradition that goes way back to Japan's feudal past.

LÉNA MAUGER
Translated by Tina Kover

A man outside a metro station in Tokyo.

He lives discreetly amid a maze of narrow streets in northern Tokyo, out beyond the railway tracks. It's an ideal place to hide or to escape to. This evening there is no moon, and the few pedestrians glide beneath neon lights, the rumble of trains giving rhythm to this shadow play.

His house stands on a corner, an anonymous white concrete cube. A simple sign on the façade proclaims 'Clearances of all types' in Japanese characters. This is definitely the place. Three vans are parked out front, men busily unloading items from them. One of them, short and thickset, steps forwards in the dim light. 'The chief should be here soon.'

It's freezing. I wait for a long time. Half an hour later the man comes back and gestures towards a staircase. The chief has his headquarters upstairs. It's a shambles: mountains of paper, maps, old computers, typewriters, walkie-talkies. Sitting behind a desk, the chief is hidden by stacks of folders. He stands up: thin, serious, impassive. He bows from the waist, greets me, introduces himself: 'Kuni Kazufumi'. Here he is at last, then, this phantom who has finally agreed to meet us after crying off several times, to tell us the story of a disappearance. His own.

Kuni Kazufumi is one of the evaporated. He left the office one day as usual, but he never again went home. Like tens of thousands in Japan, where the phenomenon of 'evaporation' goes back hundreds of years, he just vanished.

BECOMING A MAN WITHOUT A PAST

From an envelope hidden away on a bookshelf he ceremoniously pulls out yellowed sheets of paper, laying them out one by one.

Then an expired ID card. He is young in the photo, his expression betraying his ambition. His family name? Okuniya. His birth date? 16 April Shōwa 18, 1943. It's definitely him, Kazufumi. Yet the ID card describes a man who no longer exists. The skin of the face has become papery, the back stooped and the family name has lost an ideogram to become *Kuni* – a phonetic mutilation, both scar and metaphor for his life.

'How did you leave?'

'I just got on the train. It was four years after I'd started working for a securities firm, in Shōwa 45 [1970]. It was evening; I was young. I don't remember the exact date any longer.'

He stares off into space. Now sixty-six, Kazufumi allows his mind to drift back to a time when he believed the world was his for the taking. A graduate of a prestigious Japanese university, he was working as a broker in charge of managing high-risk transactions – 'I was a *topsellerman*,' he says. Stylish and full of promise, he racked up the accomplishments – until the day when, after a bad investment, he clocked

---

LÉNA MAUGER is a traveller and journalist who writes for the French magazines *6Mois* and *Revue XXI*, in which this article was published. She is the author of a book, with photography by Stéphane Remael, on the subject of the evaporated, *The Vanished: The 'Evaporated People' of Japan* (Skyhorse Publishing, 2016). A film adaptation of the book is currently in production.

> 'Here he is at last, then, this phantom who has finally agreed to meet us after crying off several times, to tell us the story of a disappearance. His own.'

a deadweight loss of '¥400 million' (c. US$3.7 million / £2.8 million). His clients bombarded him with questions, and his bosses blamed him for the transaction. 'I realised that the company was going to come down on me like a ton of bricks, so I decided to run away.' Kazufumi chooses his words carefully as he speaks, as if he's being tested. 'One evening I went and hid in the home of an old university classmate.' His friend lived in a working-class district of Tokyo. For weeks the two men shared a small apartment, living as complete strangers. Kazufumi shut himself away, not speaking. He had begun his evaporation.

In the family's native mountains his father led the investigation, putting up missing-person posters and hiring a private detective. 'My father spent a lot of time looking for me …' Debt-collectors threatened him. Eventually Kazufumi's employers realised that they couldn't 'take legal action against someone who had disappeared; on what would they have based their case?'

Kazufumi wandered, weaving in and out of Tokyo's cracks; like all capitals, the city has never been lacking in employers prepared to turn a blind eye. By turns bricklayer, labourer, dishwasher and waiter in a nightclub, he 'roamed'. 'I did all the most menial jobs. I earned ¥8,000 (c. US$75 / £60) a day. That was enough for food and a place to sleep. It also toughened me up, physically and psychologically.' The people he met now knew him as Mr Kuni, a man without a past.

In his office the telephone rings. Kazufumi answers it and then hangs up abruptly. He wants to stay focused. It takes effort to put the pieces of a broken past back together. 'I wasn't looking for a new life,' he resumes. 'I ran away, that's all. There's no glory in running away. No money or social status. The most important thing is to stay alive.' After a few years of wandering he managed to rent an apartment anonymously. Then he learned in newspapers of the existence of aid societies that provided private individuals with *benri-ya*, odd-job men or handymen. These small companies offered all sorts of services, from watering plants to walking the dog to forced evictions. Sensing a good business opportunity, at age thirty-eight the former child prodigy launched the 'Clearances of all types' company he still runs today.

He holds an official 'remover's licence' that authorises him to transport anything and everything. 'We started by collecting dead dogs that had been run over in the street. Rotting, stinking, crawling with vermin. People backed away; they couldn't bear to look. We were disgusted as well, but somebody had to do it. I didn't have a choice. It was my livelihood. That was when I resolved never to shrink from anything.'

'RUNAWAY SERVICE'
The telephone interrupts him again. Kazufumi has a hurried conversation. 'Call back tomorrow.' He continues, unperturbed, 'I also deal with hazardous industrial and electronic waste. The rest are drowned corpses, nauseating scraps of humanity. But we're at the very bottom of society, so we have no qualms.'

Kazufumi also does something else. Something secret. The very thing that has

> 'Since his own disappearance Kazufumi has helped more than a hundred men and women to vanish. He never goes looking for customers; they come to him, finding him by word of mouth or attracted by his "Clearances of all types" slogan.'

brought me to his office. His 'Clearances of all types' company also provides a 'runaway service'. Instead of cadavers, there are sometimes living bodies in his vans. Fugitives, people like him: this evaporated man is also an evaporator. Since his own disappearance Kazufumi has helped more than a hundred men and women to vanish. He never goes looking for customers; they come to him, finding him by word of mouth or attracted by his 'Clearances of all types' slogan. 'They always talk about "moving house" on the phone. But when they ask us to come at 8 p.m. or midnight we know right away what they really want.'

Not all applicants are accepted. The chief subjects them to a rigorous examination. 'My father was a police officer, and he taught me not to cross the yellow line. I don't take anyone on who seems shady.' Kazufumi rejects 90 per cent of the requests, but when an agreement is sealed, everything happens very fast. At dusk a strange crew arrives with sheets and black curtains. Windows are obscured and furniture hastily wrapped. 'The customers all say they've got no belongings, but when the time comes they want to take everything with them, including the washing machine. We're as discreet and quick as we can be.'

There is the occasional surprise. 'Sometimes I've moved entire businesses, like an erotic bookstore. In cases like that you have to be even more vigilant. You wear trainers not leather shoes. I make sure there are no hidden microphones. And, to cover our tracks, I scatter around papers with phony addresses.' Sometimes danger lurks. Some customers are armed with knives, clubs or wooden *katanas* (swords). 'D-day is very stressful; they're on edge, afraid their creditors will show up out of nowhere.' There can be fights or chases.

The evaporator's clients are single people, model salarymen (see page 174), sometimes even whole families, average Japanese citizens – men, women and children – fleeing debt owed to companies with ties to the yakuza. In debt recovery, violence is a means of convincing. Kazufumi, the launderer of shadows, is their last hope. His first piece of advice is that women and children should go somewhere safe the night before. On the day of the 'disappearance' only the men accompany him. In the night his vans carry away the distress without leaving a trace.

I ask Kazufumi if he can put me in contact with any of the evaporated. He refuses. 'I've erased them all from my memory.' He delicately reseals his large, yellowed envelope with his wrinkled fingers. The interview is over; it's time for me to leave. The door has almost closed behind me when I hear him say quietly, 'Take a look near the Mount Fuji hot springs ...'

KITSCHY, OLD-FASHIONED, LANGUID ...
The Shinkansen, an aerodynamic high-speed train, runs to the west of Tokyo at three hundred kilometres per hour. On the

The Evaporated

right is Mount Fuji, the symbol of Japan; on the left is the Pacific Ocean, gleaming and peaceful. 'Take a look near the Mount Fuji hot springs,' Kazufumi had said, and that's what I'm doing. With its winding streets, its industrial port, its concrete pier and decrepit hotels, the coastal resort of Atami is kitschy, old-fashioned and languid and is known for its *onsen*, its hot springs. The Japanese can't get enough of them.

The tradition of visiting the springs began in the seventeenth century, in feudal Japan, and continued through the late nineteenth. Throughout this period literature and theatre linked the volcanic hot springs with the fate of the evaporated ones. Innumerable books and plays recount the adventures of fugitives who come to discard their pasts in the sulphurous vapours of the *onsen* before 'reappearing' somewhere else. The most desperate purify themselves here, taking their own lives – 'total disappearance'. It is from this metaphor that the expression 'evaporated ones' – *jōhatsu* in Japanese – is drawn.

The area near the train station is busy on this Saturday. Women dressed as geishas hand out flyers for the hot springs. From behind counters grandmothers sell the specialities of the city: dried fish and redbean cakes. One of them serves grilled eels. Leaning back against her stove she speaks with pleasure of Fuji's baths. 'You should visit those at the Taikansō hotel, up there on the hill. They're the oldest in Atami, built in 1928. You just go up that street there and turn left after the bridge …'

'And the evaporated ones – are there any here in Atami?'

The grandmother turns her back, rubbing her hands together above the stove. She doesn't say another word.

At the police station the officers are resolutely silent. At the Taikansō the management dispatches an engineer in

MORE THAN A HOT BATH

Japan's *onsen* developed in the sixth century, following the spread of Buddhism, as places of purification with strong religious connotations. These hot-spring spas are found all over the country thanks to the archipelago's intense geothermic activity. Over the centuries *onsen* have changed along with society: as religious centres or spiritual retreats but also places of entertainment (or brothels) and centres for health treatment, they have had to reinvent themselves continually, and eventually became tourist destinations visited by Japanese and foreigners alike. In line with the tradition that regards *onsen* as more than simply places for a hot bath, many have shifted their emphasis from the therapeutic aspect to the experience surrounding the *onsen*, based on entertainment, shopping, good food, massages and comfort, a phenomenon that has accelerated over the past decade following a series of scandals linked to the hygiene and purity of the hot-spring waters. Other *onsen* have instead opted to focus on tradition, emphasising the close link with nature and the local community (festivals, folklore, handicrafts), the authenticity of the waters and the more spiritual aspects of bathing, focusing on the karmic benefits of the waters. One of the pioneers of this trend, Kinosaki Onsen, claims that they can help with academic success, protect travellers, prevent fires and invariably bring luck in the hunt for a soulmate.

overalls to steer me away; he pulls me beneath some distant scaffolding, clearly irritated. 'There aren't any evaporated around here,' he says, his eyes continually darting around. 'There used to be a shortage of labourers, so they'd hire anyone, no questions asked. But now they look into people, their backgrounds, their families ...' The engineer turns and walks away.

All over the city the question elicits the same sense of unease. 'We're a respectable establishment, madam,' replies the director of one *onsen*. 'Those are just stories,' says another. Only one hotel manager, huddled behind his cash register, lets anything slip. 'Dr Uchida, the physician at the springs, might be able to help you ...'

Dr Uchida runs a free clinic in the city centre. At the entrance thirty pairs of shoes are lined up, many of them quite small; this must be children's day. The waiting room is packed. After an hour Dr Uchida receives me in his surgery, an antiseptic room in which nurses are fluttering busily about. Wearing green scrubs and a surgical mask, he speaks with simplicity and honesty. 'Many Japanese come here because the hot springs of Mount Fuji have been famous for centuries. It's very rare for them to commit suicide after bathing. They usually spend several days in the city.'

A child being examined by one of the nurses starts to cry, and then another follows suit. Dr Uchida raises his voice over their cries. 'Some of the evaporated find work in the *ryokan* [inns], perhaps as housekeeping staff. It's no secret that the hot springs are a refuge for criminals and people who have fallen on hard times. The people who live here still remember when the murderer Fukuda Kazuko was on the run. She remained at large for fifteen years after killing a colleague, and the police traced her to the Atami hot springs. It was a scandal.' An assistant signals that the clock is ticking. 'If I were you I'd visit the 24-hour baths near Shizuoka ...'

Shizuoka translates as 'calm hill'. Although even closer to Mount Fuji, the city has little charm. Its seventy thousand residents live amid a sprawl of warehouses and apartment blocks; in the city centre stands a shiny new facility, the Hananoyu Onsen. In this immense leisure and commercial complex softly carpeted paths lead to restaurants, video arcades and cinemas arranged around baths. Two hours away from Tokyo, this is a paradise for the residents of the Japanese capital, who come to spend whole weekends *en famille*.

The director, Mr Uchino Taruno, is proud of his temple of well-being. He insists on showing me around personally. Dressed to the nines, straight backed in his polished shoes, he emphasises the 'heated marble' floors, the 'salt *and* sand' massages, the 'state-of-the-art' sauna and the dining room. 'May I offer you a cup of tea?' he asks. And, sinking into the red velvet cushions of an alcove, he begins to doze off, peacefully. He has to be jolted out of his drowsiness. 'Have you ever had anything to do with the evaporated?'

Mr Uchino Taruno chokes on his tea. 'Evaporated? Here? Er ...' He hesitates for a long time, trying to gather his thoughts. Then he speaks, slowly. 'It's true that we often have people who come here alone who are in the midst of a family crisis. They leave their homes not really knowing where to go. Here, the advantage is that they're unlikely to run into anyone they know. And we're open twenty-four hours a day.'

'What are their stories?'

'I don't know. That has nothing to do with me.'

Mr Uchino stands up, rearranging his suit. 'What's certain is that our treatments are good for lost souls.'

> 'For nine years he owned a moving company. He ran an ordinary business until, one evening in the karaoke bar he frequented a woman asked him to make her "disappear" with her furniture. She couldn't bear her husband's debts any more, she said. They were "ruining" her life.'

THE ESCAPE SHOP

Back to where we began: Tokyo. Kazufumi, the evaporator, mentioned a television series to me, *Yonige-ya honpo* ('The Escape Shop'). A friend loans me a DVD of these fifteen stories of evaporation written against a backdrop of suspense and chaotic action. The show drew record audiences in the late 1990s. In the series, characters who have gone bankrupt disappear – but always after comical plot twists and high-speed chases with the mafia. One of the heroes, the owner of a runaway service, made a particular impression on Kazufumi. This alter ego, mobile as a ninja, jubilantly guaranteed his clients that they would always 'reappear'.

The show's scriptwriter agrees to meet me in Shinjuku, in the bar of a four-star hotel with sweeping views of the capital's ultra-modern cityscape. At sixty years old, Hara Takahito is the archetypal producer who appears to have been fighting tooth and nail against the ageing process: deep tan, impeccable loafers, teenage-style bracelets. He bubbles over with enthusiasm for everything, laughing and clapping like a child. It was after writing and directing three feature films about people who vanish that he decided, he explains, to create a series for television. 'I wanted to highlight a problem the media doesn't dare talk about. Independent loan companies are controlled by the mafia. If debtors don't pay on time, the yakuza puts pressure on them that can extend all the way to murder.'

THE EVAPORATOR

Hara Takahito loves grand, expansive gestures. He also loves to get fired up. 'The bursting of the financial bubble was a tragedy. No matter the size of their debt, borrowers killed themselves. Entire families committed suicide, but many people decided it was better to go on living with a different identity. *Yonige* is an ancient phenomenon; it became popular in the 1990s.' In Japanese, *yo* means night and *nige* to run away. *Yonige* means a secret escape leading to disappearance.

To bring this social phenomenon to life the screenwriter drew on various facts and accounts. 'Our fiction is very realistic,' he insists. During the research on which he based his scripted situations, Takahito had long discussions with an evaporator, bringing the man out of the shadows and into the light of day. The man wrote a book based on his life. Takahito gives me his telephone number.

The author is delighted at my call. His name is Hatori Shō. He is forty-one years old. In 1997 he published *Za yonige-ya* ('The Runaway Agency'). I meet up with him several hours later in Yokohama. He's waiting for me in the glitzy foyer of a hotel and steers me immediately to the bar.

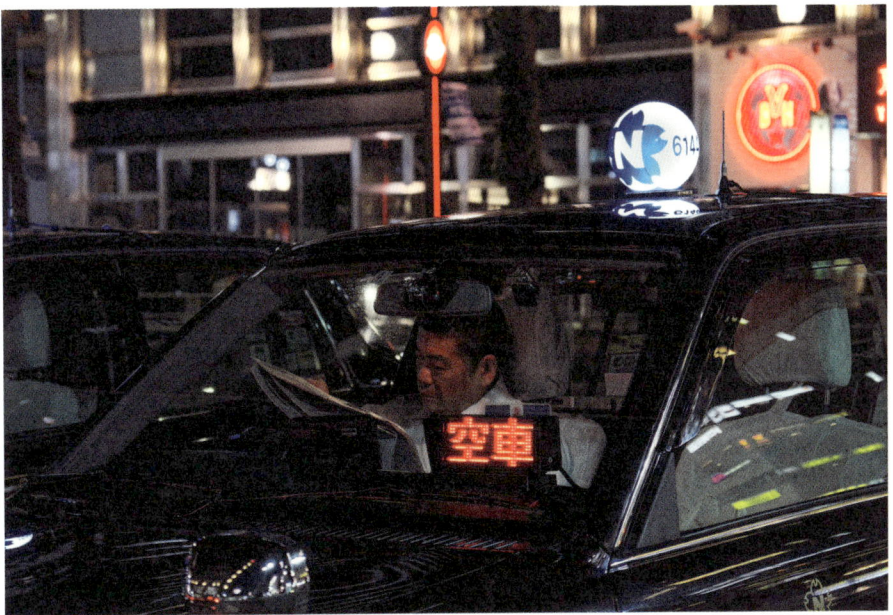

Above and pages 163, 164, 167: Night-time views of the Shibuya district of Tokyo after midnight.

Short, muscular and sharp featured, Shō looks like a yakuza: same silver chain, same black jacket, same wary expression. For nine years he owned a moving company. He ran an ordinary business until, one evening in the karaoke bar he frequented a woman asked him to make her 'disappear' with her furniture. She couldn't bear her husband's debts any more, she said. They were 'ruining' her life. Shō took the job. It was a success.

The business owner smelled a golden opportunity. He published an advertisement: 'House moves at night'. Just a 'wink', he assures me today. It was the period when the financial bubble was bursting, and 'immediately' Shō was 'deluged with customers'. He decided to take on the role of saviour, bringing together hired men and fugitives in his office, sketching plans on a whiteboard, looking for the best hideouts, imagining every possible scenario. His 'night jobs' cost ¥400,000 (c. US$3,650 / £2,850), three times the price of an ordinary house move. He churns out ghosts as if on an assembly line.

Shō received numerous calls from women – '*office ladies*' addicted to buying clothing and luxury brands, swimming in debt. Wives abused by their husbands. Young graduates who, lodged by their bosses in large dormitories, were being exploited and couldn't take it any longer. None of them could admit their troubles to the police or their loved ones. Better to run away than lose face. 'I would urge them to hang in there, but they fled anyway.'

The publication of his memoirs brought him widespread public recognition. He was the subject of articles in Japan, the United States and Europe. In each one Shō presented himself as a 'writer, producer and manager' and insisted that, just like on television, his vanished ones are living happy lives. He likes to think of himself as an example. 'People often associate *yonige* with cowardice, but doing this work has helped me understand what healthy behaviour is.'

At the end of the interview he calls over his seventeen-year-old daughter, a karate champion in a pleated skirt. He wants to make her into a 'movie star'. It will be his revenge for his own past. He is an evaporated person, too – or rather, a 'child of evaporation'. His own family fled Kyoto when he was a small child. Debt ... again.

'LIKE MAKING THE DEAD TALK'

Dinner this evening is at a noisy, overheated restaurant in the Shibuya district on Tokyo's west side. Between dishes of raw fish washed down with sake, a journalist brings up the question of the evaporated. Half curious, half disbelieving, people around the table come to life. A Japanese university professor wonders, 'How can they be unearthed? By finding their families; why not? But, the disappeared ... even the police can't manage that.' A photographer jokes, 'It would be like making the dead talk.' Another diner thinks aloud, 'We've all heard stories about people who have vanished, but from that to finding them again ... Maybe it's enough just to mention it.' The professor steps in, 'Sorry, but we're very reserved. We don't just show up at each other's homes; we don't display our emotions.

With a taboo like disappearance, I doubt you'd find that ...'

And yet, they are out there, everywhere. A painter and mother of two children who has spent twenty years waiting since the day she went as usual to the restaurant owned by her husband to cover the lunch service and another man greeted her instead – her husband had just sold the place without telling her and vanished. She's had no news of him since. 'Sometimes I think my husband is wandering in San'ya, the part of Tokyo where the dropouts go.'

There is also the quiet, reserved schoolgirl whose father ran away fifteen years ago leaving behind his papers, his keys, everything. Twice the girl thought she'd spotted him in the street. An elusive silhouette, vague memories. If she had caught his eye, would she have spoken to him? No. She 'detests' her father. She has never made any effort to find him.

'WE USED TO LIVE AMONG THE CHERRY TREES'

The families of the evaporated have nowhere to turn. In Japan adults have the legal right to disappear. It's an accepted reality, a given. 'When someone disappears we simply say "*shō ga nai*", which means "nothing can be done about it". I wasn't around during the Edo period, but even back then, when something serious happened, people resigned themselves to it,' recalled Hara Takahito.

The fate of the Kurihama family is illuminating. They are hidden away far from chain restaurants and hotels, in a working-class neighbourhood northeast of the capital. Mikio, the father, opens the door. Moustached and paunchy, wearing an oversized woollen sweater, the 61-year-old former bricklayer looks like a trade unionist. In the family's main living area – a poorly heated kitchen crowded with

> "'In this house *yonige* has become a taboo word. As if we were pariahs. But who can say now that they've never wanted to – and never will want to – change their lives?'"

wobbly dressers, piles of dishes, knick-knacks, dolls, snow globes and children's drawings – he pulls up a few mismatched chairs. Seconds later his quiet wife, a postal employee, comes home from work.

The atmosphere is tense, the silence difficult to break. The oldest son, Thim, stands stiff and unmoving in front of the table, staring fixedly at the patchwork of salvaged carpet on the floor. Lying in bed upstairs the partially disabled grandmother clears her throat. Mikio and his wife sit facing each other across the table.

'We used to live among the cherry trees in Saitama, on the Kantō Plain.' With these words, Mikio begins his journey through the past. The son of leather-workers, he became a kendo instructor at the age of twenty, a notable achievement for a man of low caste: kendo is the swordplay of the samurai. A respected man, Mikio taught evening classes to police officers. The martial-arts master wed Tomoko in an arranged marriage. The couple learned to love each other and, in the 1980s, set their hearts on opening a *gyōza* restaurant. Mikio borrowed some money. He won't say how much.

The restaurant struggled to attract customers, and the country, affected by the economic crisis, sank into recession. It became impossible to make the loan repayments. Mikio and Tomoko began to fear for the family's safety. 'It would have taken a century to clear those debts.' Tomoko was pregnant with Thim, their first child. Mikio's mother shared the couple's home. It was she who made the decision to sell the house quietly and leave everything behind.

One 1 January, a day of celebration and storms, the Kurihama family evaporated.

Thim is still standing, still unmoving, still rigid. He is the only child who has been allowed to share the secret. This evening his brothers, who have grown up with the lie of an idyllic past – cherry trees in blossom, the lovely house, the 'voluntary departure' for Tokyo – have been sent to a friend's house. But Thim has stayed. 'He's a mystery to us,' says Mikio. 'He's like the calm surface of a lake with unknown, hidden depths. The other two are easier to understand; they're doing well at university.' Thim, with his pierced lip, remains frozen. 'I think I've put too much pressure on him,' says Tomoko suddenly, putting a kettle on the fire with a clatter and attacking a heap of dirty dishes.

'THROW IN THE TOWEL'

Mikio has grown tense. He fiddles nervously with the arms of his glasses. Suddenly, the pain he has kept contained until now bursts out, 'In this house *yonige* has become a taboo word. As if we were pariahs. But who can say now that they've never wanted to – and never will want to – change their lives? People are cowards. They're inevitably tempted to throw in the towel, to disappear and reappear some place where no one knows them.'

Tomoko sits back down, the dishes abandoned. Mikio stares at the flowers on the plastic tablecloth. 'I never thought of running away as an end in itself. My mother taught me to overcome obstacles and to fight. But disappearing meant giving myself a chance to be reborn, cleansed of my flaws.'

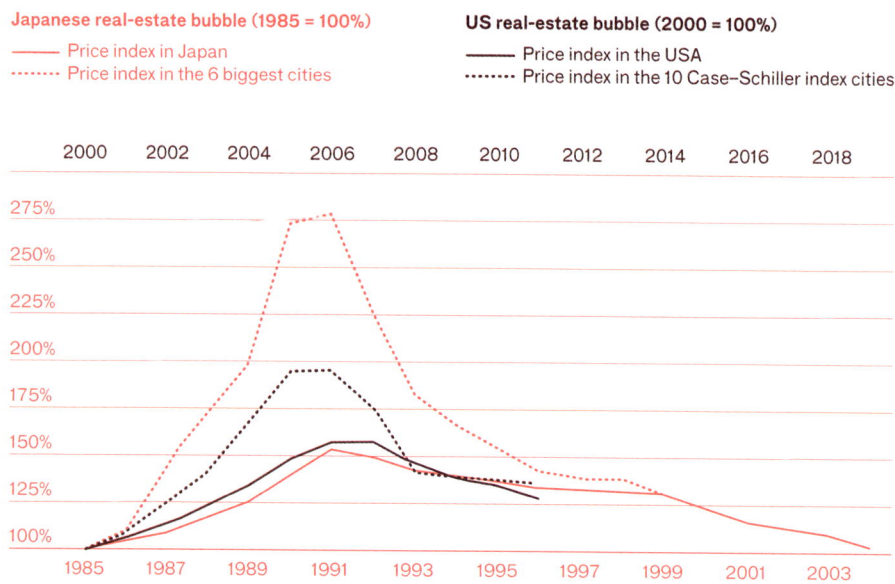

JAPANESE AND US REAL-ESTATE BUBBLES COMPARED

THE LOST DECADE

In 1987 Japan overtook the United States in terms of per capita income. Two years later the Nikkei index (the stock market index for the Tokyo Stock Exchange) reached its historic high, and people thought that Japan would soon become the world's leading economy. But there were clear signs of a giant bubble: it was said that the Imperial Palace in Tokyo (not that it was for sale!) had a real-estate value equivalent to the whole of California. In the early months of 1991 the bubble burst, sending house prices tumbling and cutting the value of the Nikkei index by more than a half. The country fell into a crisis marked by low growth and deflation known as the 'lost decade', although it has lasted much longer than ten years, and its effects continue to be felt. Unemployment remained relatively low, but calculations show that between 1995 and 2007 real salaries fell by 5 per cent while prices remained stagnant. Domestic consumption has never returned to 1980s levels, and the companies that dominated their sectors back then, such as Toyota and Sony, have found themselves competing with Korean rivals. In response to chronic deflation and low growth Japan has tried to stimulate the economy by accumulating a net public debt equivalent to 153 per cent of GDP, which is the highest level in the world (even though most of it is held in the domestic market and by the central bank). In reality, the economy's low growth rates are in part the result of an ageing society: if you look at per capita income for the working-age population, Japan saw higher growth levels in the 2000s than the USA and many European countries. It has also remained the world's largest creditor country.

> "'I never thought of running away as an end in itself. My mother taught me to overcome obstacles and to fight. But disappearing meant giving myself a chance to be reborn, cleansed of my flaws.'"

The father's guilt is clear. 'I'm aware of my own weaknesses. For example, I wanted to back out of our meeting today. It's not easy to spill your guts, and what good does it do you? But I told myself it was a new challenge I was facing. Disappearance is something that clings to you, you know. Running away means running towards death.' Thim closes his eyes. His father keeps talking. 'I'm tired, but I keep to my path, and I have no reason to change my life any more. I only want one thing: to live in peace with my wife and my children. Until the end.'

Mikio stands up in the heavy silence. 'Do you still practise kendo?'

'No, but my sons have taken it up!'

More at ease now, he pulls a photo album from a nook and leafs through it. Thim goes to a cupboard and brings out a collection of long-stashed-away medals and trophies. Ten minutes later Mikio slips out and then makes a dramatic entrance. Thim says, admiringly, 'You look like a yakuza, Papa!' Dressed in loose trousers and indigo jacket, a metal-mesh mask covering his face, Mikio wields a sharp sabre with ease in this small room. He has put on his kendo uniform for the first time in twenty-three years. Upstairs the grandmother grumbles. She wants to be here for this and has to be helped down the stairs. Mikio places her gently in a dilapidated chair in the middle of the room. The old lady gazes at her son nostalgically.

I go back to see Kazufumi, the evaporator. His experience is invaluable. He, the professional, knows very well that 'reappearances' rarely happen the way they do in the movies. How can anything be built on a lie? Kazufumi has not managed it. He married but never told his secret to his wife. The marriage failed.

Like many ghosts, Kazufumi has never registered with the authorities in his new area of residence – and as far as those in his home city are concerned, he has officially disappeared, thus losing all his rights. No social security. No school either for children of the evaporated. 'In Japan they don't keep track of us as much as in your country. It's easy to disappear.' To remain in his parallel world, Kazufumi lives in an administrative no-man's land.

His office is covered with sketches. 'I mainly move people from one place in Tokyo to another. It's easy to vanish in the anonymity of the capital. But I also relocate some customers to the countryside.'

Sōda Shunsuke is one of the 'relocated'. He is one of the thousands of unemployed and disillusioned residents of supercities who have quietly moved to repopulate the rural areas. The forty-something man who comes to pick me up from the train station in a sports jacket has retained the stylish appearance of a city dweller. His hands are pale and smooth, his car spotless. Shunsuke left Tokyo seven years ago for the province of Yamanashi in northern Japan. He drives fast, in spite of the fog. Forests and rolling fields flash past the car windows. He doesn't stop until we reach a dirt road at the foot of a wooded hill.

Standing in the mud, he points out four large plastic greenhouses. 'Spinach in the winter; tomatoes, lettuce and strawberries in the summer.' A couple of farmers in mud-encrusted boots are picking lettuce on the neighbouring parcel of land. They stare at Shunsuke. 'They never say hello to me. I'm not a real market gardener to them. They don't trust me.'

SHUNSUKE, THE ROOTLESS MAN
It begins raining heavily. There is no shelter nearby. Shunsuke doesn't want to go to his house – 'It's a long way from here, and I have to deliver my vegetables ...' He gets back into the car. 'I used to be a salaryman like all the ones you see in Tokyo, stressed out, subservient to their companies. I worked in a very large hotel, ten to twelve hours a day. I thought I was losing my mind.' In the car Shunsuke spins his tale. At his wits' end, he learned that there was a need for labourers in the countryside. He chanced it, registering for a six-month agricultural training course at a university in northern Japan. Now all he had to do was finance his move. 'My father is very rich, but I didn't want to owe him anything. Since I didn't have any collateral to get a bank loan, I went to a title company.'

'You mean a loan shark?'

'You know Japan well!'

The interest rates were too high. Shunsuke couldn't pay back the money. Another failure. Evaporation became unavoidable. 'I took the most important things first, and then the movers came in a truck for the rest.' With the remains of the loan he rented a small apartment, a tractor and some tools. Then he set to work, hard. The winters are harsh and the loneliness considerable, but, in his greenhouses, the rootless man feels more at peace. It is only then, reluctantly, that Shunsuke admits to *yonige*.

THE RISE AND FALL OF THE SALARYMAN

The Japanese term salaryman (or *sararīman*), is a pseudo-Anglicism referring to a male employee of a large company. In the post-war period, being a salaryman equated to recognition and stability: employment more or less guaranteed until retirement, with initially low salaries that rose predictably in a pay structure based on seniority rather than merit. In exchange, the salaryman devoted his life to the company: long working hours, unconditional loyalty, evenings spent entertaining clients. So the salaryman came to stand for modern Japan: the white-collar hero who created the world's second-largest economy from the ashes of the Second World War. Nowadays, however, in the wake of the economic crisis of the 1990s that led to redundancies and fixed-term contracts, scaling back the post-war social pact, the salaryman has become a sad or ridiculous figure in the collective imagination: the absent father and husband, the conformist with a boring job offering little satisfaction, the company slave, the drunk asleep on the metro.
A generational change is under way, and many younger people are refusing to put work at the centre of their lives.

Illuminated office windows in a building in Tokyo's commercial district.

He parks in the courtyard of an attractive modern house. A strange thing: he said he lived in a small apartment. An older man in his seventies wearing slippers appears on the doorstep. 'My father,' says Shunsuke. The man bows and goes back inside. His wife, waiting in the vestibule, has fetched a pair of slippers for each of us. The parquet floors are gleaming, the decor bourgeois and Western. Everything is sleek and orderly.

In perfect English the father invites me into the living room. 'I was a director at Mitsubishi. I'm retired now, but I often do projects for large companies.' His elegant wife brings coffee and biscuits. 'This place is our second home. We had it built last year. Before that, we used to go to a hotel. But a house is much more comfortable. And our son can enjoy it. It's better for him here than in his little apartment, don't you think?' Shunsuke sits listlessly on the sofa, his arms crossed tightly like a child after a quarrel.

'Mr Sōda, are you happy with your son's career change?'

'I could never have done it myself. Working the land isn't for me. But Shunsuke is young and healthy. Here he eats well, he exercises … it might make things more complicated when he reaches retirement age, but I have confidence in him. He'll be all right.'

Mr Sōda makes a mock-playful grab at his son's shoulder. Shunsuke recoils. 'Of course, I was surprised when he told me he wanted to become a farmer, but I've always supported him. Haven't I always supported you?' The father is speaking for his son now. 'He needs to find a wife. Not easy in this backwater … nothing but peasants.'

It's time to leave. A last energetic thump on Shunsuke's back, a few steps to the front door. Mr and Mrs Sōda watch the car until we are out of sight.

'I don't understand. Do you live with your parents?'

'No, I told you, I have an apartment. But it's small and it's not very homely. My parents insisted on following me.'

Sulkily, Shunsuke explains that he wanted to 'reassure' his parents after four years of silence. Without asking any questions his father soon had the new house built. The farmer explodes. 'I feel like a man on the run yearning for a normal life. I thought I'd managed to put a little distance between us, but I failed. My father is overbearing and intrusive.'

THE LAW OF SILENCE

Kazufumi believes that silence should be maintained for at least five years. The evaporator himself went for fifteen without calling his parents. He was afraid. Afraid they would refuse to speak to him; afraid they would be in poor health; afraid they had received threats because of him. They forgave him. Kazufumi never felt strong enough to see them again, but he felt less guilty.

Where their parents remain silent, some children of the evaporated speak out. Like Hatori Shō, the writer who inspired the TV series about the vanished. And then there are the others, those who can't face up to their pasts: the nameless, the lost, the losers, the ones who have had their memories amputated. Many of them end up in San'ya, not far from Kazufumi's house.

San'ya is the haunt of common labourers, criminals and the homeless. This city-within-the-city is reached by metro, and metro only. According to local associations, 70 per cent of the population may be evaporated. But they aren't telling their stories. The only law in San'ya is the law of silence. It takes several trips to convince Norihiro.

Norihiro is fifty years old. His face is

> 'Norihiro is a false name intended to "fool the police". "After all this time I could reclaim my identity, of course. That's what evaporated ones do who start over, who begin a new life. But I don't want my family to see me like this. Look at me. I don't just look like nothing; I am nothing."'

bloated by sake, his baggy clothes somehow emphasising his emaciated form. He suggests that I come with him through the streets of small furnished bedsits and dilapidated buildings to his shabby hotel. Men sitting on cardboard boxes tease him. 'You getting it on with foreigners now?' The door to his room is padlocked; its walls windowless and bare. There are no personal effects, no papers. Just stubbed-out cigarettes and a tattered tatami mat.

'I don't just look like nothing; I am nothing'

Each morning at dawn Norihiro waits in front of a bungalow for the hiring bosses to arrive. But work is scarce. The economy is in crisis, and the most vulnerable are being affected. The mafiosi who employ day labourers are less powerful now, too. Alcohol, exhaustion, fatality, *giri-giri* life (existing in conditions just barely adequate for survival), Norihiro is no stranger to any of them. 'There are thousands of men like me in San'ya. Unpaid debts, hopelessness, pressure at work, arguments; it's normal. But I see more and more young men killing themselves.'

Norihiro is a false name intended to 'fool the police'. 'After all this time I could reclaim my identity, of course. That's what evaporated ones do who start over, who begin a new life. But I don't want my family to see me like this. Look at me. I don't just look like nothing; I am nothing. If I die tomorrow I don't want anyone to be able to find me.'

Aged forty, a handsome man with a wandering eye despite his devotion to his wife, Norihiro was a brilliant engineer. Abruptly fired one day, he kept to his old routine. As he did every day, he put on his suit and his leather shoes and went out the door, briefcase in hand. His wife wished him a good day, resting a hand on his shoulder. He waited in front of his old office building all day without speaking or eating. He carried on this way for a week. 'I couldn't bear it any longer. I even waited past seven o'clock, because that was when I used to go drinking with my bosses and my colleagues. I just wandered, and when I finally went home I felt like my wife and son were suspicious. I felt guilty. I no longer had any salary to give them ...'

On pay day Norihiro shaved, kissed his wife and took the same metro line. But in the other direction. At the end of the line: oblivion. 'It hurts to think that my parents looked for me. I hope they're doing well. Maybe they still think I'll come back. Maybe they're dead.' Of his wife and son Norihiro says nothing. 🖋

The names of some individuals and places have been changed.

The Iconic Object: The *Woshuretto*

If you visit Japan it won't be long before you see one – and it's an encounter that will change your life.

GIACOMO DONATI
Translated by Jennifer Higgins

We're not talking about Godzilla or about the life-size Gundam models. No, this is the human, all too human, *woshuretto*, or *washlet*, otherwise known as the Japanese toilet, an extraordinary creation that incorporates toilet, bidet and more besides. On first coming across one of these, the question inevitably springs to mind: a vision of the future or pure madness?

A little bit of background. Japan is a country where space is at a premium, particularly in the cities, which house 91.7 per cent of the overall population of around 127 million. Except for the very rich or those living in the countryside, the only way of finding enough room to live is to be crammed together in dwellings that can seem like bits of larger houses rather than proper living spaces or in densely populated apartment blocks. Here, each apartment is the size of a few tatami mats, and every square millimetre of space has a specific function. Futons are brought out of cupboards each evening and disappear back into them the next morning, freeing up precious space. This explains why, as anyone who has been to Japan knows, everything is in miniature: fridges, ovens, microwaves, bathtubs. For the majority of the population this isn't a question of taste or preference but of necessity – a way of avoiding being suffocated by their domestic appliances, feeling like guests in their own homes.

It's a continuous process of reduction, a merciless battle of liberation, a credo that sends the sanest of people reaching for the latest book by the organising consultant Kondō Marie in search of perfect order, with every corner inexorably salvaged from chaos. At the same time, as any good Japanese person will tell you, there can be no concessions to immaculate hygiene.

The concept of cleanliness is everywhere in Japanese life. Schoolchildren clean their classrooms, people look after the street in front of their houses and even throughout their whole neighbourhood: they prune trees and sometimes clean public swimming baths. There is no litter whatsoever, partly because there are no litter bins and almost everyone goes out with

a little bag for their rubbish, which is then taken home to be recycled. And anybody can treat themselves to the pleasure of a daily soak: if people haven't got a shower or the more traditional tub for indulging in the cleansing and relaxing ritual of *ofuro* – post-washing immersion in very hot water – then for a few yen they can visit one of the countless public baths.

It was in the early 1960s that the typically Japanese preoccupations with space and cleanliness came together in one unique, extraordinary idea that was to alter the lives of millions of Japanese people. Some bright sparks at Toto, the company that had first introduced European-style toilets into the Far East, picked up on a Swiss invention that had hardly been exploited, even in the USA. They updated its technology so that it met the standards of a country in the middle of an economic boom. Two decades and several failed attempts later, in 1980 a new creation came into being; love it or hate it, it was impossible to be indifferent to it: the first model of the *woshuretto*.

Initially, despite considerable curiosity about this new discovery, it failed to catch on, but eventually, ten or so years later, it became impossible to ignore the smiles on the faces of the first *woshuretto* pioneers, and orders skyrocketed. Today it is estimated that almost three out of four families have one. Basically, they're everywhere.

It does everything except make coffee. There's even a control panel on the side with dozens of buttons that are impossible to figure out even armed with a dictionary.

A first visit to one of these means pressing buttons at random just to make it do the most basic things, but, with a bit of practice, you can really have a ball: there's the bottom cleaner, the women-only bidet function, the heated seat and the rinse mode – and that's only the start. The fun really gets going with warm air for drying, music to cover the most embarrassing moments, dignity-preserving deodorant, pulsating jets of water, disinfectant spray, seats that automatically lift if you go anywhere near them, rinses that leap into action the moment you rise from your throne … but those are just the basic functions. The control unit on the most sophisticated model boasts thirty-eight buttons: it's mind boggling.

The feeling when you try it for the first time must be similar to what the astronauts felt when they first got into the Apollo. The welcoming warmth of the 38-Celsius seat, the first murmurs of the contraption getting going, the feeling of sitting on a jet engine rather than a bog-standard toilet, the nervous hope that it won't explode, the rinse that sucks everything away like a mighty whirlpool and then the final thrill beside which everything else pales: the embarrassment of the water jet that emerges just when those of us used to washing as a separate activity least expect it. And the subtle pleasure that ensues.

Nothing is as it was before. It's a reverse baptism. A welcome that, when you get on the plane home, you find yourself missing. Because only when you've experienced this can you say that you've felt, even just for a moment, Toto-lly Japanese.

The National Obsession: Blood Types

Among Japanese culture's many 'idiosyncrasies', few are as inexplicable as the passion for blood types. Characters in anime and video games are always given a specific type, and they are seen as key identifying features of actors and singers: any interview will feature a question about blood type, alongside the usual ones about favourite foods, colours and animals. But the interest doesn't end with fictional characters or celebrities. The well-worn phrase '*Ketsuekigata nāni?*' ('Which blood type are you?') is a common ice breaker, rather like the Western 'What's your star sign?' The reason for all this? There's a widespread conviction that blood type is somehow linked to personality.

What is the origin of this belief that doesn't exist anywhere else in the world? In 1927 Furukawa Takeji, a professor at a women's university in Tokyo, published an article entitled 'The Study of Temperament Through Blood Type'. Furukawa had no medical or scientific training, and the theory was on the shaky side, but it still had a huge impact on its readers. In the years that followed the Japanese Army even tried to apply it to its training methods, dividing soldiers up according to their blood type (to no noticeable effect). By 1933 the idea had already been discredited by several research studies, and its popularity quickly died.

All that changed in 1971. A book called *Ketsueki-gata de wakaru aisho* ('Understanding Affinity Through Blood Type'), a manual setting out possible blood-type combinations between couples, became a bestseller. Its author was Nomi Masahiko, a journalist with an engineering degree and no medical expertise, who skilfully revived Furukawa's theories. Nomi successfully got blood from a stone, producing a ten-volume literary sensation and planting the idea of the four blood-type personalities firmly in the Japanese psyche. This resulted in a tide of manuals and diets devised for specific blood types and dating agencies promising perfect compatibility. Companies frequently asked new employees to specify their blood type, and there were many alleged cases of bullying and 'blood-type harassment' (*burahara*), usually targeting the unfortunate Bs. There is now a ban on specifying blood type on CVs. This is why:

MATTEO BATTARRA
Translated by Jennifer Higgins

TYPE A
Precise, serious, trustworthy, they tend towards good harmonious relationships with colleagues. It comes as no surprise to learn that this is the commonest type in Japan. However, they are often shy and easily become stressed.

TYPE O
Optimistic, extrovert, self-confident, they can make great leaders and friends. They aren't always punctual or attentive to detail.

TYPE B
Impulsive, unpredictable and very creative, they are, however, seen as the black sheep of the four types. They are perceived to be selfish, egocentric and stubborn.

TYPE AB
The rarest blood type in Japan. A combination of A and B, resulting in a sort of split personality: reserved but friendly, restrained but expansive. Overall, the classic manga hero who seems cold and distant at first but who turns out to have a big heart.

Despite having been repeatedly discussed and discredited over the years, the theory remains firmly rooted in Japanese culture. Try going to amazon.jp and type in 血液型 (blood type). Thousands of books and manuals will pop up. If you do the same on YouTube you'll also find an amazing cartoon series in which the characters are animated blood types.

Some people have come up with anthropological explanations for this phenomenon, reminding us that blood has always had an important place in traditional Japanese culture, particularly in the transmission of hereditary characteristics. Others see psychological and social reasons: the Japanese tend to perceive themselves as a rather uniform population and seek ways to differentiate themselves from one another. Another clue might be in the fact that the distribution between blood types is fairly equal: around 40 per cent A, 30 per cent O, 20 per cent B and 10 per cent AB. It is not surprising that negative characteristics are attributed to a minority type (the Bs), while the As are seen as the 'true' Japanese (although surely this was just a case of needing to sell as many books as possible?). The ABs are even rarer and thus have a joker-like status.

In reality, though, people know full well that the whole business has no scientific basis and see it as a largely harmless obsession. So why not try it for yourself? Evaluate your relationship with your own partner according to the number of antigens in your red blood cells. Here's a summary of the most common combinations (I refer you to the internet for a world of possible variants).

<u>A and O:</u>	an excellent partnership with complementary strengths
<u>A and B:</u>	a bad combination of opposites
<u>B and B:</u>	very risky if the partners are very different from one another
<u>AB and AB:</u>	odd, but can work well
<u>B and O or AB:</u>	flexible and open, they go well together
<u>AB and O:</u>	better as friends than lovers

The Phenomenon: J-Pop

CESARE ALEMANNI
Translated by Jennifer Higgins

All over the world, sales of CDs and vinyl have been decimated by online piracy and legal streaming services such as Spotify, but one successful chain, Tower Records Japan, is bucking that trend with its enormous stores. While in many parts of the world businesses like this are struggling just to get by (the original US Tower Records filed for bankruptcy in 2006), in Tokyo, Tower Records is not just surviving but prospering. The store in Shibuya is one example: seven floors of discs. Each floor – covering hundreds of square metres of floor space – is dedicated to a particular genre and teems with hundreds of Japanese who still, well into the twenty-first century, see CDs and vinyl as something worth spending money on. The desire to collect things, coupled with a liberal dose of nerdy perfectionism, is a significant feature of contemporary Japanese culture.

One of the most crowded floors is given over to a kind of music most favoured by (but not only by) teenagers: J-pop. This genre – if it can be called that – is Japan's most popular and most exported and is the driving force behind the country's record business, one of the most successful in the world. The Japanese music industry's annual turnover is almost US$3 billion (72 per cent of which comes from disc sales), making it second only to the US market, with its annual US$5 billion turnover (of which only 15 per cent comes from sales of CDs and vinyl).

Go into the J-pop section of any Tower Records, and you'll find a scene that has been unfamiliar to those in the West for some years now: swarms of kids with flashy hair and clothes thronging noisily around the discs and merchandise, for all the world as though the internet didn't exist. The walls are covered with posters showing the youthful faces of girls and boys, unnaturally luminous thanks to excessive Photoshopping. These are the idols of J-pop.

J-pop isn't only the most successful musical genre in Japan it's also one of the most difficult to explain to somebody who doesn't know about it. While on a purely musical level it is exactly what its name suggests – lightweight, commercial, fashionable music – everything else about it is far less straightforward.

The genre could be described as blending *kayōkyoku* (traditional pop music), British and American pop-rock and new wave. In the early 1990s several J-pop producers realised that the best way of maximising the commercial success of their groups was to create them artificially, controlling every detail, from the music to the looks and personalities of the musicians. This is why J-pop stars are 'bred' rather like battery hens in special academies to become idols (*aidoru*) perfectly adapted to each new generation of adolescents. This is the case of, for example, AKB48, a girl group from the Akihabara district of Tokyo that has sold over 56 million records since 2005. Managed as a constantly expanding group, AKB48 had 130 members by 2015, all young women between the ages of fifteen and twenty, each one held to a contract that sets limits on their public and private behaviour. Such contracts commonly require members to remain single. This is because a good *aidoru* needs to be 'pure' so that female fans can identify with her but also 'free' in order to fit the fantasies of the male fans. Breaking this rule can have serious consequences. Minegishi Minami knows something about this: she is one of the most prominent members of AKB48, and in 2013 a tabloid newspaper accused her of having spent the night with Shirahama Alan from Generations, another *aidoru*. Minegishi found herself at the centre of a media storm. She was demoted within the group from being a 'leader' to an 'apprentice' and had to apologise in a YouTube video in which, in an act of public contrition, she appeared in tears with her head shaved.

In this sense, J-pop is reminiscent of the Western phenomenon of boy bands that flourished in the second half of the 1990s, the difference being that, whereas boy bands now represent the exception rather than the rule among stars of Western music, Japanese J-pop idols are still being created in an endless cycle. There are limitless numbers of them, and they manage to win over most Japanese teenagers, who don't seem to mind the fact that there is little that is spontaneous in the music they grow up with and that – as Minegishi's case showed – their idols must fulfil their fans' fantasies by living in a prison that is barely gilded.

An Author Recommends

A book, a film and an album to understand Japan, chosen by:

FURUKAWA HIDEO
Translated by Polly Barton

One of the most highly regarded figures in contemporary Japanese literature, Furukawa Hideo has received the Mystery Writers of Japan Award, the Japan SF Grand Prize and the Mishima Yukio Prize. Among his titles translated into English are *Belka, Why Don't You Bark* (Haikasoru, 2012), *Horses, Horses, in the End the Light Remains Pure: A Tale That Begins with Fukushima* (Columbia University Press, 2016) and *Slow Boat* (Pushkin Press, 2017).

THE BOOK
SENNEN NO YURAKU ('A THOUSAND YEARS OF PLEASURE')
Nakagami Kenji
1982

Borrowing the Indian term 'caste' for describing social strata, we could say that from the late Middle Ages onwards Japan had a strict caste system and that, as in India, there were individuals who existed outside of such castes – the 'outcastes'. These outcasts were designated as the targets of extreme discrimination and suffered oppression as a result. Nakagami Kenji, author of this book, came from a regional community inhabited by such outcasts – a fact that he himself made public, although only after establishing a reputation for himself as an author. It should be said that Nakagami Kenji is a truly brilliant writer, and in *Sennen no yuraku* ('A Thousand Years of Pleasure') that brilliance of his appears in condensed form. The book tells the profoundly dreamlike story of a village midwife who delivers 'just about every child born'. This is an outcast village, and here beautiful young men are born, have their fill of sex and violence, then meet a rapid downfall – which is to say, they die young. Their deaths are repeated, over and over. In other words, what we find here is a continual cycle of reincarnation. The midwife around whom the narrative revolves is illiterate. Accordingly, she simply records for herself in her mind, 'by memory, the lives of all kinds of people'. This is, simply put, an oral history. So what does it mean for this oral history to be written down, to be made into a book? Isn't that a contradiction in terms? Nakagami asserts fervently that it isn't. People are born and people die. People are discriminated against, and yet they are as beautiful as anyone else in society. As it happens, Japan now has just one caste, together with the people who are outside of that caste, namely the emperor and his family. This was all apparent to Nakagami as he dreamed his thousand-year-long dream. Unfortunately this title has never appeared in English translation, but a number of Nakagami's other books have, including: *The Cape and Other Stories from the Japanese Ghetto* (Stone Bridge Press, 1999) and *Snakelust* (Kodansha International, 1999). A film based on the book, directed by Wakamatsu Kōji, was released in 2012 and given the English title *The Millennial Rapture* for international release.

An Author Recommends

THE FILM
TYPHOON CLUB
(Original title:
TAIFŪ KURABU)
Sōmai Shinji
1985

Is adolescence the same the world over? How will a film about Japanese teenagers appear to foreign audiences? To tell you the truth, I can't really imagine. What I can say is that for the Japanese (by which I mean the average Japanese person), adolescence is like the period immediately before an explosion. When I say explosion, I mean in terms of sex – and also awareness of death. This film, directed by Sōmai Shinji, is a true wonder – and it's utterly persuasive in its portrayal of adolescence as that period when 'while having not yet come into contact with sex or death, you're more directly in touch with the essence of those things than someone who's had sex a hundred million times or someone who's experienced death once (which is to say, a dead person)'. The film's protagonists are at middle school, aged fourteen or fifteen – in other words, standing clearly on the cusp between their early and late teens. They live in a somewhat provincial area, a little way away from Tokyo. Here we see the contrast between Japan's largest metropolis and the farming regions of endless fields that surround it. This contrast comes together with that between the childishness one is permitted in one's early teens and the maturity one is judged to have from the age of fifteen onwards. Some of the film's characters have problems at home; some are tortured by feelings of love from which they have no means of escape. There is a notable absence of adults around them who could serve as role models. And, that autumn, a typhoon ravages Japan, that island country in the Pacific they call home. This natural disaster serves as both tragedy and liberating force. Such disasters are always tragedies and forces of liberation. The film's characters go wild; some cross a line from which there is no return. This is what a truly amazing film looks like – at least, that's how it seems to me.

THE ALBUM
UNIVERSAL INVADER
Newest Model
1992

It was because Japan was a caste society, a society of discrimination, that the samurai were able to build the country that they dreamed of – and, in fact, Japan has always lacked a feel for diverse elements being thoroughly mixed together. This is linked to the survival of the imperial system, with the emergence of regional communities that are discriminated against (the outcasts) and also to contemporary Japanese society, which drives its teenagers crazy. Has Japan really not found a way through all this? This band appeared to show otherwise. Newest Model formed in 1985 and split up in 1993. The Japanese term 'mixture rock' – used to describe rock fused with other genres – perfectly describes their music. And, with *Universal Invader*, their final album, they truly did mix everything up. In the opening track, for example, the lyrics are in equal parts English and Japanese, swapping between the two. Up to that point there had been experiments in moving away from Japanese within pop music – singing the bridge in English, for example, sometimes the entire song – but here we find the clear expression of a philosophy that says very simply, 'Why not just go half-and-half?' Moreover, the music itself can only be termed a kind of *rock monster*. By monster, I mean something that grabs the tones, the melodies, the beats from all manner of other genres, mixes them up and scatters them everywhere. It's really satisfying stuff. When they realised what they'd achieved Newest Model had no choice but to call it a day, but that doesn't take anything away from the importance of their experimentation.

An Author Recommends

The Playlist

Listen to this playlist at:
open.spotify.com/user/iperborea

FURUKAWA HIDEO
Translated by Polly Barton

I have absolutely no idea what kind of Japanese pop music is popular in other countries, but my guess is that the songs and artists on this playlist are unlikely to be considered particularly important. That's because innovators almost never provide for 'the masses'. They reject popular ideals and instead serve the individual. They offer the individuals in whatever age they're living through in Japan ('me' and 'you', who are living at this moment) something into which they've invested their souls. Of course, there are exceptions to this rule. On this playlist, Inoue Yōsui is regarded as one of the gods of Japanese pop (a huge success, someone whose name is never far from the adjective 'super'), and Asian Kung-Fu Generation continue to be the forerunners in the world of Japanese rock (they now have endless imitators). And yet, there are many other groups who are their equals. Or, in some cases, there *were* such groups or artists, but they've split. What unites all these is that they've changed the mental landscapes of all the individuals who listen to them in Japan. It's those landscape-changers who are the true innovators.

1
Newest Model
'Chishiki o ete, kokoro o hiraki, jitensha ni nore!'
1991

2
Friction
'Replicant Walk'
1988

3
Number Girl
'Teppū, surudoku natte'
2003

4
Tha Blue Herb
'Phase 3'
2007

5
Nakamura Kazuyoshi
'Inu to neko'
1997

6
Yura Yura Teikoku
'Yura yura teikoku de kangaechū'
2001

7
Asian Kung-Fu Generation
'Love Song of New Century'
2010

8
Endō Michirō
'Okāsan, iikagen anata no kao wa wasurete shimaimashita'
1984

9
Supercar
'Strobolights'
2001

10
Inoue Yōsui
'Kōri no sekai'
1973

11
Quruli
'Tokyo'
1998

12
Clammbon
'Surround'
2001

Further Reading

FICTION

Furukawa Hideo
Slow Boat
Pushkin Press, 2017

Kakuta Mitsuyo
The Woman on the Other Shore
Kodansha International, 2007

Matsumoto Seichō
A Quiet Place
Bitter Lemon Press, 2016

Miyamoto Teru
Inhabitation
Counterpoint Press, 2019

Mori Ōgai
Gan
One Peace Books, 2014

Murakami Haruki
1Q84: Books One, Two and Three
Vintage, 2012

Murakami Ryū
Coin Locker Babies
Pushkin Press, 2013

Murata Sayaka
Convenience Store Woman
Granta Books, 2019 (UK) /
Grove Press, 2019 (USA)

Ogawa Yōko
The Housekeeper and the Professor
Vintage, 2010 (UK) / Picador, 2009 (USA)

Yoshida Shūichi
Villain
Vintage, 2011

Yoshimoto Banana
Asleep
Faber and Faber, 2001 (UK) /
Grove Press, 2001 (USA)

NON-FICTION

Ian Buruma
A Japanese Mirror
Atlantic Books, 2012

Will Ferguson
Hitching Rides With Buddha
Canongate, 2006

Matt Goulding
Rice, Noodle, Fish: Deep Travels Through Japan's Food Culture
Hardie Grant Books, 2016 (UK) / Harper Wave/Anthony Bourdain, 2015 (USA)

Christopher Harding
Japan Story: In Search of a Nation, 1850 to the Present
Allen Lane, 2018

Igort
Japanese Notebooks
Chronicle Books, 2017

Alex Kerr
Lost Japan: Last Glimpse of Beautiful Japan
Penguin, 2015

Léna Mauger with Stéphane Remael
*The Vanished: The 'Evaporated
People' of Japan*
Skyhorse Publishing, 2016

Richard Lloyd Parry
People Who Eat Darkness
Vintage, 2012 (UK) / Farrar, Straus
and Giroux, 2012 (USA)

Susan Napier
Miyazakiworld: A Life in Art
Yale University Press, 2018

MANGA

Murata Yūsuke
One-Punch Man
VIZ Media, 2014 onwards

Noda Satoru
Golden Kamuy
VIZ Media, 2017 onwards

Oda Eiichirō
One Piece
VIZ Media, 2003 onwards

Taniguchi Jirō
A Distant Neighborhood
Fanfare, 2016

Tatsumi Yoshihiro
A Drifting Life
Drawn and Quarterly, 2009

Tatsuta Kazuto
*Ichi-F: A Worker's Graphic Memoir
of the Fukushima Nuclear Power Plant*
Kodansha Comics, 2017

Tezuka Osamu
Message to Adolf: Parts One and Two
Vertical, 2012

Urasawa Naoki
20th Century Boys
VIZ Media, 2018 onwards (reprint edition)

Further Reading

Graphic design and art direction: Tomo Tomo and Pietro Buffa

Photography: Pietro Masturzo
The photographic content is curated by Prospekt Photographers.

Illustrations: Edoardo Massa

Infographics and cartography: Pietro Buffa

Thanks to: Giorgio Amitrano, Matteo Battarra, Alessandro Borini, Gianluca Coci, Giacomo Donati, Gala Maria Follaco, Fukuda Toshihiko, Flavia Fulco, Federica Lippi, Tania Palmieri, Francesca Pellicciari, Matilde Presotto, Cristina Rendina, Sekiguchi Ryōko, Yonemura Fumiko

The opinions expressed in this publication are those of the authors and do not purport to reflect the views and opinions of the publishers.

http://europaeditions.com/thepassenger
http://europaeditions.co.uk/thepassenger
#ThePassengerMag

The Passenger – Japan
© Iperborea S.r.l., Milan, and Europa Editions, 2020

Translators: French – Tina Kover (The Evaporated); Italian – Katherine Gregor (editorial, The Mythbuster, The Number, photographer's biography, Of Bears and Men), Jennifer Higgins (sidebars, Family Album, The Iconic Object, The National Obsession, The Phenomenon), Alan Thawley (sidebars, author biographies, standfirsts, picture captions); Japanese – Polly Barton (An Author Recommends, The Playlist), Meredith McKinney (The 'Do-It-Yourself' Women, A Simple Thank You, The Withering of Desire).
All translations © Iperborea S.r.l., Milan, and Europa Editions, 2020

ISBN: 9781787702196

All Rights Reserved. No part of this publication may be reproduced, stored in a retrieval system or transmitted in any form or by any means without the written permission of the publishers and copyright owners.

The moral rights of the authors and other copyright-holders are hereby asserted in accordance with the Copyright Designs and Patents Act 1988.

Printed on Munken Pure thanks to the support of Arctic Paper

Printed by ELCOGRAF S.p.A., Verona, Italy

Ghosts of the Tsunami
© Richard Lloyd Parry, 2014
First published in the *London Review of Books* Reproduced by permission of the author c/o Rogers, Coleridge & White Ltd, 20 Powis Mews, London, W11 1JN, UK

The 'Do-It-Yourself' Women
© Sekiguchi Ryōko, 2018

The (No Longer So) Secret Cult that Governs Japan
© Jake Adelstein, 2018

Why Japan Is Populist-Free
© Ian Buruma, 2018

A Simple Thank You
© Yoshimoto Banana, 2013
First published in *Shimokitazawa ni tsuite*

The Withering of Desire
© Murakami Ryū, 2010

Of Bears and Men
© Cesare Alemanni, 2018

Sea of Crises
© Brian Phillips, 2014

Sweet Bitter Blues
© Amanda Petrusich, 2016
First published in *Oxford American* magazine, 2016

Family Album
© Giorgio Amitrano, 2018

The Evaporated
© Léna Mauger, 2009